THE
WESTERN
KINGDOM

THE BIRTH OF
CORNWALL

THE WESTERN KINGDOM

THE BIRTH OF CORNWALL

JOHN FLETCHER

The
History
Press

First published 2022

The History Press
97 St George's Place, Cheltenham,
Gloucestershire, GL50 3QB
www.thehistorypress.co.uk

British Library Cataloguing in Publication Data.
A catalogue record for this book is available from the British Library.

ISBN 978 1 8039 9000 2

Typesetting and origination by The History Press
Printed and bound in Great Britain by TJ Books Limited, Padstow, Cornwall.

Trees for LYfe

CONTENTS

INTRODUCTION

This book is the result of around seventeen years of research and passion for the Early Medieval history of Cornwall and the south-west. It began when I arrived at the University of Plymouth as a teenaged undergraduate. Already a keen Viking reenactor, I thought it might be fun to look into the regional history of Devon and Cornwall.

That passing whim ended up sending me down a rabbit hole, tracking down the often elusive and widely scattered hints of a history that was much more fascinating than it was ever given credit for. The availability and accessibility of that history has come on leaps and bounds since then. Books like *The Promontory People* by the late Craig Weatherhill throw a much-needed spotlight on the era, while the number of Cornish finds on the Portable Antiquity Schemes online catalogue has increased year on year.

This work is an attempt to pull together some of this new research, as well as older works that have not been given their proper due, and present not only a new timeline of Cornish history over the Early Medieval period but also how these events helped to shape and preserve Cornwall's unique identity.

That identity is one of Cornwall's biggest draws. It sometimes feels like Cornwall is in fact two different places. One is the present-day duchy; a land of pleasant beaches, hilly fields and holiday homes that features fondly in the memories of many people throughout the UK but which nonetheless seethes with an undercurrent of conflict between those who enjoy visiting each summer and those who often struggle to live in those same sunny villages.

The other Cornwall seems more mythological, the realm of Arthur and of Giants, where Mesolithic monuments sit astride modern farmers' fields which have been laid to the same plan for thousands of years. There is much that is great and fascinating in this past, but it always seems perhaps just out of reach; something that is teased at but which shifts out of sight when one tries to focus on it.

Of course, each of these Cornwalls is tied inexorably to the other. The mystery and mystique of Cornwall is as much a draw to visitors as the spotless beaches, while the modern handling of Cornish affairs, the dilution of its identity and complex history to being just another of England's counties and the complicated web of economic issues forcing many of its young people abroad all serve to further hide and obscure its past.

What can't be ignored is that, whichever Cornwall one finds oneself in, Cornwall feels different. Despite its long inclusion in the English state and the pressures of a sometimes violent history, there is still an unmistakable Cornish identity that can be felt. It makes itself known in the black and white Baner Peran flying from houses and town centres and in the oddities of speech and language, even the occasional smattering of revived Cornish language heard on the street and in cafes.

The question then becomes where does this identity come from? Is it the product of nineteenth-century revivalists or does it harken back to something older, something in that mythological past that still makes itself felt in the present?

To answer the question, as is so often the case with questions of national identities in the British Isles, one must look at the Early Medieval period; those centuries between the end of Roman rule in Britain and the coming of the Normans in 1066. Over this crucial period were forged both the concepts of individual peoples – the English, the Scots and the Welsh – as well as the borders of nation states that we would recognise today.

Cornwall and the Cornish are also among them, and preceding them, and the story of how Cornwall changed from the heart of the great western kingdom of Dumnonia into its own independent Kingdom of Kernow, then finally became part of Wessex and the wider English state, is a tale not only of battles and bloodshed but of diplomacy and compromise.

Crucially, it is a story about survival. About how, when defeat and annihilation seemed perhaps inevitable, the Cornish found a way to bend with the storm and in the process kept their unique language, culture and history well into the modern era.

This book attempts to tell that story, pulling together evidence from documentary, archaeological and other sources to shed light on the often half-remembered history of Cornwall's past. It is inevitable in such an undertaking that some evidence may be missed or that others may come to their own conclusions. Ultimately I can only hope to present the results of my own research and let the reader decide on the merits of the case I lay out.

A couple of final notes regarding the descriptions used for Cornwall's opponents and eventual allies. I have tended to discuss the Germanic incomers to Britain as Anglo-Saxons or Saxons. This is a simplification of the complex origins of the immigrants. However, it is one I still believe is widely recognised and therefore has merit for the ease of both the writer and reader.

Finally, I should warn the reader that this book will deal only lightly and briefly with the Arthurian mythos. These stories have, in the centuries since their initial inception as a Brythonic superheroic figure and eventual transformation into romantic epic, become undeniably linked with Cornwall and the south-west. However, the shadow of Arthurian legend has a tendency to consume all it comes in contact with and has, at times, severely hindered the work of understanding the Western Kingdom as it was, rather than how a poet may have wished it to be.

Certainly there is every indication that tales of Arthur may have echoed around the halls of a Cornish lord in the centuries we will describe. However, we shall keep him in that fantastical realm as it suits him best.

PART 1

SETTING THE SCENE: POST-ROMAN BRITAIN AND THE WESTERN KINGDOM

1

RUIN AND CONQUEST? CHALLENGING TRADITIONAL NARRATIVES

The Early Medieval period, still commonly (and erroneously) referred to as the 'Dark Ages', has often been painted in the harshest possible tones. It appears in the minds of many people as a time when civilisation faltered; a dark slide into barbarism and chaos that only the glories of the Enlightenment halted and eventually reversed.

For the British Isles, this story goes, the Roman legions left and chaos descended. The rich villas and cities the Romans had built were abandoned, warlords appeared everywhere, and then marauding bands of Germanic invaders arrived and swept all before them in a terrible tide of violence and flame. Within a generation or two the Romano-Britons were driven to the west and over the sea, seeking refuge in Brittany, while the new Saxon kingdoms sat dominant over what would become England.

This picture has, thankfully, been slowly disproved thanks to the efforts of archaeologists and historians over recent decades. However, while academic discourse has moved away from marauding hordes of invaders into more detailed debates about exactly how and why the material and linguistic culture of the Romano-Britons was replaced, at least in England, by the Germanic culture of the people we now call Anglo-Saxons, this is still the popular view of the period.

We will discuss some of the current debate further on in the chapter. For now, it is worth understanding some of the key points of what we'll call the 'traditional' view of the Adventus Saxonum, or coming of the Saxons, as the Venerable Bede named it, as well as the sources that helped formulate it.

Before we get into that, though, it may be helpful to state what we do know about this, the beginning of the Early Medieval period (or Late Antiquity, as Ken Dark [Dark, 1994] and others have referred to this early portion).

In the late fourth and early fifth centuries, the remaining imperial Roman forces in Britain, already weakened by a series of ill-advised expeditions by would-be British emperors, were withdrawn. This process may have begun earlier in the west of Britain than in the east and south-east, as suggested by Frere [1987] and others, but regardless by around a decade into the fifth century there were no longer any significant Roman forces in Britain. More than that, the bureaucracy and logistical innovations that helped the empire run were also absent and, in the power vacuum they left, the power of local elites experienced rapid growth.

As the fifth century continued, there were increasing numbers of raiders and settlers entering Britain from both 'Germanic' regions (mainly Southern Denmark and Northern Germany) as well as from Ireland. There may also have been increasing conflict with the Picts, who had always dwelt beyond the empire's borders in modern-day Scotland.

I say that we know the above because these, the most bare-bones descriptions of events that would have been momentous and life-changing for those in the midst of them, are attested in multiple sources or have archaeology to support them. For the detail – the how, why and who that flesh out this timeline – we have to look to sources, and unfortunately for a long time these sources have been both limited and poorly utilised.

From this relatively sparse base came the idea of invasion and replacement, aided by the few finds of archaeology that can be definitively described as 'Romano-British' rather than 'Saxon'. Of course, part of the problem with this is that the Saxons, at least when they first arrived, were a pagan people practising furnished burial customs. This means we have more of their goods to discover in the first place. Secondly, the crossover between goods traditionally described as Roman and those described as Saxon is now thought to be much broader than previously considered, meaning someone buried with a 'Saxon' brooch may in fact be a fashion-conscious Briton.

In terms of first-hand sources, as in contemporary accounts of events in Britain at the end of Roman rule, we have none. The closest source, and thus considered the primary account for many years, is that of the Briton priest Gildas. Sometime between the end of the fifth and the mid-sixth century (Guy Halsall places it around 540 [Halsall, 2013]) he wrote *De Excidio et Conquestu Britanniae* (*On the Ruin and Conquest of Britain*) a sermon intended to shame and condemn the rulers of Britain at the time he lived, as well as including a history of events leading up to his own time.

Gildas' account contains much of the meat behind which the traditional narrative is formed. He describes a Britain beset by Anglo-Saxon invaders whose rulers have lost God's favour and, as such, brought down all the many woes upon themselves.

It is, of course, also notable as one of the bedrocks of Arthurian myth, providing the earliest mention of a possible 'King Arthur' in the form of Ambrosius Aurelianus and describing a Briton victory over the Saxons at Mount Badon, as well as other touchstones such as Vortigern and the invitation of the Saxons to Britain.

Due to its near-contemporary date and the dearth of other sources, Gildas was, for many years, read and quoted with confidence as a true account of the events he is describing without receiving the scepticism some of his writings perhaps deserved. This has, of course, not been the case with more recent scholarly analysis, but as he is fundamental to the traditional narrative it is important to understand how he was used and (less frequently) is still used. His opening remarks set the tone for the wider work:

> Whatever in this my epistle I may write in my humble but well meaning manner, rather by way of lamentation than for display, let no one suppose that it springs from contempt of others or that I foolishly esteem myself as better than they; for alas! the subject of my complaint is the general destruction of everything that is good, and the general growth of evil throughout the land; – but that I rejoice to see her revive therefrom: for it is my present purpose to relate the deeds of an indolent and slothful race.

While this quote is undoubtedly among the most severe, it is not overly exceptional in its tone from the rest of the *De Excidio*. Gildas was, after all, not interested in writing a dispassionate history but rather in condemning what he perceived as the moral failings of his contemporary kings.

A sometimes underappreciated reason Gildas forms such an essential bedrock for students of this period and why he was clung to so strongly is that his chosen narrative, a great empire being undermined and punished for failing to meet a perceived moral standard, could hardly have been better formed to appeal to the sensibilities of the Victorian historians. As Vance [1997] noted, history was, to the mind of these Victorians, a place to mine for allegory in order to extol the chosen virtues of the historian even if it required a selective or even ahistorical reading of the sources. In Gildas' case, his fiery almost Old Testament-inspired rhetoric could not have hoped for a more receptive audience.

It is these historians who are responsible for forming the picture of British history that was taught in schools for generations. This is particularly true of the Early Medieval period as the Victorians found much to admire in stories of doughty Germanic invaders restoring order and civilisation to a chaotic land. This has had numerous impacts on the field, not least of which is the enduring tendency for studies of this period to focus firmly on the English or Anglo-Saxon experience.

So if we cannot take what Gildas has written at face value, is there anything we can gain from his writings?

Yes, but ironically much of what can be divined from his work would run counter to the narrative he, and many of his early interpreters, wish to put forward.

To begin with, and perhaps most crucially, the *De Excidio* is a written work. Not merely written, but written in a form and style of Latin which makes clear that Gildas had access to a full education in both the language and the tropes and mores of its classical use. This means that, as late as the closing years of the fifth century, there were still places of education within Britain, likely monasteries and other Christian establishments, capable of providing such an education. Indeed, we can see from other sources, such as the recent find of a seventh-century windowsill from Tintagel ['Second inscribed stone found at Tintagel', *Current Archaeology*, 2021] bearing the remains of some practice writing evidently done casually, almost as though doodling, that literacy remained present in post-Roman Britain for centuries after the end of the empire. This runs directly counter to the picture Gildas himself is trying to put forward, as well as that of the traditional viewpoint which postulates that all signs of civilisation are swept aside with literacy amongst them.

Gildas can also be a useful source to give some insight into the political landscape of Britain in his day. As mentioned, the real purpose of *De Excidio* isn't to give a dispassionate historical account but rather to rail against the native elites of his time. To this end Gildas lists several rulers of Britain to single out for condemnation. He also paints a picture of a Britain fractured into a number of smaller polities, rather than a single unified Romano-British state. As Gildas puts it:

> Kings Britain has, but they are as her tyrants: she has judges, but they are ungodly men: engaged in frequent plunder and disturbance, but of harmless men: avenging and defending, yea for the benefit of criminals and robbers. They have numerous wives, though harlots and adulterous women: they swear but by way of forswearing, making vows yet almost

immediately use falsehood. They make wars, but the wars they undertake are civil and unjust ones.

Again his penchant for fiery rhetoric is likely painting a worse picture than may have existed but at its heart he appears to be describing an Early Medieval society such as we may recognise from the Continent or from the Mid-Saxon period of the Heptarchy. This is a world dominated by lords and kings of smaller polities and their bands of warriors. For the native Britons these bands were the Teulu (pronounced *Tay-Lee*) or 'family', a group of likely noble warriors gathered around a senior lord who followed him into battle and enacted his will. We will return to these bands and their role in warfare in a later chapter.

Returning to Gildas, his defamation of the kings is also notable because it gives us one of our first post-Roman mentions of Dumnonia, the Western Kingdom that emerges in the south-west of Britain following Roman withdrawal, with lands stretching from Land's End to the Somerset levels and perhaps beyond. There is some debate about the periods occupied by, in the first instance, the Durotriges, and then by Dumnonia and Wessex. Specifically, Gildas states:

> Of this so execrable a wickedness Constantine, the tyrannical whelp of the unclean lioness of Damnonia, is not ignorant. In this year, after a dreadful form of oath, by which he bound himself that he would use no deceit against his subjects, making his oath first to God, and secondly to the choirs of saints and those who follow them, in reliance upon the mother (the church), he nevertheless, in the garb of a holy abbot, cruelly tore the tender sides of two royal children, while in the bosoms of two revered mothers – viz., the church and the mother after the flesh – together with their two guardians.
>
> And their arms, stretched forth, in no way to armour, which no man was in the habit of using more bravely than they at this time, but towards God and His altar, will hang in the day of judgment at thy gates, Oh Christ, as revered trophies of their patience and faith. He did this among the holy altars, as I said, with accursed sword and spear instead of teeth, so that the cloaks, red as if with clotted blood, touched the place of the heavenly sacrifice.

A number of items are of interest in this passage when examining the history of the Western Kingdom. In the first instance, it's intriguing that Constantine appears first among the kings that Gildas wishes to chide. It may be that the above incident – which we have to assume, given the extremely specific nature of it, was better known in Gildas' day – was so heinous that it moved him to strike there first. However, it may also reflect a degree of importance or power attributed to Dumnonia that has not previously been appreciated. We should consider that Maelgwn, another of the kings, is recorded as being 'Last in my Writings, First in Wickedness' and introduced with a considerable description of both his power and military success.

Also interesting to note is how Constantine is introduced: as 'the whelp of the unclean lioness'. The implication of a powerful and influential mother behind the Dumnonian king is a tantalising prospect. However, Gildas uses lions and lionesses liberally in his work, and while sometimes he seems to intend to reference specific people (the 'Lioness' Revolt' in his history is usually interpreted as a reference to Boudicca's revolt) he also used it to refer to regions, specifically calling the Saxon homelands 'the lair of the savage lioness'. On balance there is not enough information to argue definitively for either option; however, even the prospect of a lost Cornish Athelflaed-type character is exciting to imagine.

The actual symbolism Gildas uses here is also of note. Many of the kings are referred to using biblical animals such as lions, bears and dragons, and these come heaped with specific symbols in Christian iconography [Durandus, 1906], both for what they represent and for their eventual fates. The lion, at least in the Early Medieval period, is often a symbol of martyrdom and the Devil (for example: 'Thou shalt walk upon the asp and the basilisk: and thou shalt trample under foot the lion and the dragon', *Psalms* 90(91):13). This can be seen most clearly in the use of lions in Early Christian writing to exaggerate their persecution in the Colosseum; events which modern scholarship largely denies ever took place. As such, associating Constantine with lions was effectively accusing him of being in league with the Devil or, more broadly, being 'the enemy' to God and the Christian Church.

Again, we are left without enough context to be sure, but given the strident accusations being levied it is possible Gildas is identifying both Constantine and Dumnonia as an 'other' even compared to his other targets.

As for the incident itself, there seem to be some contradictions in the account. For example, where Gildas describes the victims as children but states that 'none were in the habit of [wearing armour] more bravely than they at this time'.

He also seems to deliberately conflate the idea of children being torn from their mothers' arms with his long-running symbolism of the Church as a mother. One is left with the impression that this incident, which so enraged Gildas, may have been the ending of a dynastic power struggle. Perhaps Constantine's victims were younger siblings with a better claim to the throne (given the potential insult to his mother, and bearing in mind similar incidents in the Anglo-Saxon period, it's not inconceivable that he could have been an illegitimate child) who had retreated into the church for sanctuary only to be torn out and killed. There are some similarities between this interpretation and the story of the Saints Dredenau, commemorated in a chapel to Saint Geraint in Brittany, who were supposedly Dumnonian nobles murdered by an ambitious uncle. It's worth noting that this chapel is only a few miles away from a church Gildas himself is supposed to have founded, so it's entirely possible he would be aware of the story.

Still a brutal tale, yes. But not entirely out of the ordinary for the power struggles of both the Early and Later Medieval period.

Moving on from Gildas, there are only a handful of other sources close to the events of the early fifth century that are available to us. Perhaps the most famous, or certainly the most commonly taught, is the 'Rescript of Honorius'. Commonly understood as the Emperor Honorius telling the Britons to 'Look to your own defences' in 411, this is often cited as a potential end point for Roman Britain. The simple statement, and the implied abandonment of the Romano-Britons to their fate at the hands of incoming Germanic, Irish and Pictish barbarians (those never subject to Roman rule), is often cited as further evidence for the collapse of society after Roman rule.

However, there are problems with this simplistic narrative, starting with the source itself. The Rescript comes to us through the Greek historian Zosimus, a functionary in the Eastern or Byzantine Roman Empire in the sixth century. His *History* is a work trying to capture the reigns of the Roman emperors from Augustine until the early fifth century.

Zosimus' writing is far drier than Gildas', striving to be something of a more scholarly history rather than a moral polemic. However, he was translating other sources, many from Latin, into Greek and there are reasons to believe some errors may have slipped in during this process.

For one thing, the section of his *History* which includes the Rescript is by far the most chaotic of the six books, leading some to question whether he perhaps died before he had a chance to edit his early draft. Additionally, the copy we have of Zosimus is not complete, missing several pages and perhaps the majority of the final book, wherein much of the detail regarding Britain is found.

Putting these items to one side, even Zosimus seems unsure about the fate of Britain. He notes several revolts by the legions in Britain putting various pretenders forward for the imperial throne and then murdering them just as rapidly, until Constantine III is proclaimed emperor and then leads a successful overtaking of Gaul, bringing most of his troops with him. From this event Zosimus ascribes a great deal of woe not directly relevant to our discussions.

Of more interest to us is that in 409, Zosimus describes the Britons, in response to the chaos on the Continent and under pressure from Picts and other raiders, throwing off their imperial allegiance and acting in their own defence:

> The Britons therefore took up arms, and incurred many dangerous enter-prises for their own protection, until they had freed their cities from the barbarians who besieged them. In a similar manner, the whole of Armorica, with other provinces of Gaul, delivered themselves by the same means; expelling the Roman magistrates or officers, and erecting a government, such as they pleased, of their own.

It's interesting to note here that Armorica is mentioned along with the Britons, the region essentially relating to Brittany. We will return to this later in the book.

Certainly this description seems to fit within the wider context of Zosimus' work. The Western Roman Empire of the late fourth and early fifth centuries was a chaotic place, besieged with competing forces trying to claim imperial titles and facing multiple large-scale barbarian incursions from beyond the Rhine. In such a context, and with the prospect of invaders on their own doorstep, it follows that the Britons may have decided that the costs of their four-centuries-old Roman identity – chiefly taxes in goods and manpower lost to hopeless expeditions beyond the Channel – were far outweighing the benefits that were becoming sporadic at best (such as coinage) or non-existent at worst (protection from external threats).

However, it seems strange if we consider the Rescript in its traditional role, as the response of Honorius to a desperate plea from the Britons. What could have happened in two years that took them from victorious and independent from Rome to suddenly desiring a return to the imperial fold?

With this in mind, the Rescript itself is perhaps worth revisiting, and this has been the subject of much academic discussion in recent years. It is extremely telling, for example, that the section of the *History* that the Rescript appears in is, for the most part, dealing with events on the Italian peninsula and is separated by several paragraphs from the earlier descriptions of events in Gaul and Britain.

Additionally, it is far less a clear statement ('Look to your own defences') than it is just one section of a longer description of Honorius' actions:

Honorius, having sent letters to the cities of Britain, counselling them to be watchful of their own security, and having rewarded his soldiers with the money sent by Heraclianus, lived with all imaginable ease, since he had acquired the attachment of the soldiers in all places.

Given the context of the whole statement (it's preceded by actions of the invading barbarians in Italy), and its less strident tone, it is reasonable to argue, as others have, that here we are seeing a mistranslation or mistake on the part of Zosimus, with the region in question actually being Bruttium in Italy. If true, and it certainly seems extremely likely, this robs the traditional view of one of its bedrocks.

The final source we will look at is the tales of Saint Germanus of Auxerre. Germanus was a one-time Roman governor who became the Bishop of Auxerre and then, at the urging of the Pope, undertook a mission to Britain in the late 420s to combat the Pelagian Heresy. The story of this mission, and a potential second trip of uncertain date, are recorded in two main sources. The first, the *Vita Germanus*, is a hagiography of the saint's life produced by his disciple Constantius around 480, so well within living memory of the events described. The second is the *Historia Brittonum*, often credited to Nennius but potentially of unknown author, written in the ninth century. Both of these sources are not strictly histories; the *Vita* is written expressly with the goal of honouring the saint and describing his many miracles and works, while the *Historia* is practically a mythology in itself, containing many wild tales from start to finish.

With that said, the story of Germanus can still inform our view of Britain in the fifth century and as such should not be discarded out of hand. The heresy he was sent to combat is not, in itself, of great interest to us today, it being largely a dispute regarding the nature of human morality and the importance of original sin. What is of interest to us is that the Church felt secure enough to send two prominent bishops (Germanus and Lupus, Bishop of Troyes) into Britain after the collapse of the Western Empire in order to counter the growth of undesirable doctrine. This visit is confirmed by another near-contemporary source, Prosper of Aquitaine.

The fact of the visit not only tells us something about the relative stability (at least for churchmen) in Britain, but also that goings on amongst the islands were still relatively common knowledge on the Continent, thus suggesting that trade and communication had not been completely disrupted, although they must have been impacted, by the retreat of Roman power from Britain.

Indeed the *Vita*, which is by far the more sober of the two sources (though it is jam-packed full of miracles, as is the nature of such saints' lives in the period) is full of receptive crowds of people and journeys to many towns. The impression in general is of a country not unduly different from the one they had left, albeit in the grip of a dire threat to its spiritual health.

At a debate with the Pelagian bishops, again a fairly cultured pastime for a country we have been told was awash with troubles, Germanus is able to win the day with his rhetorical skill (and another miracle), thus proving the superiority of the Catholic Orthodoxy. Following this, he undertakes more fantastical journeys around the island, including driving off a marauding army of Picts and Saxons by rousing his men to shout 'Alleluia' and as such not having to strike a single blow.

The battle, while clearly ahistorical, does provide another useful snippet for our purposes. It makes clear that there were at least some military confrontations between Britons and these groups, and that the situation was common knowledge by the 480s. While doubt can be sown around the specific event described, or about whether Constantius had any first-hand knowledge of such events in the first place, it is clear he expected his audience to at least know these basic details in order to lend his story credibility.

After this event, the *Historia* goes even further, containing many tales of Germanus sparring with Vortigern until holy fire descends from heaven, further cementing the account as more mythology than history.

A second visit is mentioned in both sources; however, this visit has proven controversial amongst historians [Barrett 2009, Thompson 1984] with the obvious parallels to the first visit making it seem like a 'doublet' to the first rather than a completely separate event. As such, we won't go into it here.

We can see from these sources that the old view of chaos, cultural loss and barbarian hordes has many problems, even in its more modern incarnations, and the events of the fifth and sixth centuries are often grossly oversimplified in order to smooth the narrative. That being said, there are commonalities in the sources which also cast doubt on the opposite side of this debate. It seems clear that there were invasions of some kind, marked by military confrontation, in both Germanus' and Gildas' time, and it formed a central issue for the Britons in both these ages.

In the absence of the traditional narrative, we now need to look at what we can establish to replace it, and specifically how these momentous events impacted the people of south-western Britain and the kingdom they formed in the absence of Rome.

2

Dumnonia: Expansionist and Wealthy

Once we move away from the written sources, it becomes clear that nowhere in mainland Britain less resembles the traditional chaotic wasteland then the south-west. In Somerset and Dorset the Durotriges seem to re-emerge around the same territory they occupied in the pre-Roman years, while further west, in Devon and Cornwall, the Kingdom of Dumnonia appears.

Dumnonia corresponds to the tribal lands of the Dumnonii, whom the Romans encountered when they first invaded in the first century. The continuity in naming between the pre-Roman tribe and the post-Roman kingdom is one very prominent sign of the level of continuity in identity that occurred during the Roman years. Indeed, Roman remains, at least in terms of buildings such as villas or large towns, are relatively scant west of Exeter (Isca Dumnorum to the Romans), suggesting that the overall level of 'Romanisation' was fairly low, particularly amongst the lower levels of society.

Where Roman remains are found these are often legionary camps or defences, such as those recently unearthed at Calstock near Plymouth, often situated where either they controlled major transport routes, or near mine works themselves, as is the case with Calstock.

Tin was vitally important to the Roman economy, both as a solder for other items and as a key component in both bronze and pewter, which the Romans used in large volumes. However, its extraction and refinement in the Roman and Early Medieval periods was a complex undertaking which required specialist skill and experience. Given this, it is perhaps reasonable to think that the Romans would consider much of the extraction best left to the local experts.

So long as the tin flowed the way the empire demanded, and the relevant taxes were paid, it is unlikely they would have profited greatly from disrupting local elites and systems, much of which would have grown up around the tin trade as a primary economic resource.

The Dumnonii had been trading tin for thousands of years by the time of the Roman invasion. It has been theorised that the Casseritides or 'Tin Isles' of Herodotus were an oblique reference to both Britain in general and Cornwall in particular. This is further supported by recent research into a number of Late Bronze Age tin ingots from the eastern Mediterranean [Berger et al., 2019] that confirmed a Cornish origin for the ingots. This strongly suggests that Cornwall formed one of the primary, if not the primary, source for tin throughout the European Bronze Age. Recent soil analysis supports this view, with continuous extraction of tin resources evident from the pre-Roman period onwards [Meharg et al., 2012].

The trade would have made the Dumnonii extremely wealthy and, along with their defensive position and geographical size, fairly powerful in pre-Roman Britain. However, there is no particular record of conflict during the Roman invasion – thus contrasting sharply with the situation in both Wales and Dorset where the Durotriges fiercely resisted Roman rule and were crushed. This further supports the idea that the Roman takeover was perhaps more amicable in the south-west than we tend to think. Roman chroniclers are never shy of telling us about victorious campaigns against barbarians, so the deafening silence around the south-west suggests that the Dumnonii elite saw their survival, and the maintenance of at least some of their power, through obedience and trade with Rome rather than military resistance. This would also fit in with what we know of other British tribes, with even Boudicca's Iceni originally agreeing to shared rule with Rome until the death of her husband and the resulting abuse by the Roman governor.

This, of course, doesn't mean that the Dumnonii, as the years of Roman rule continued, didn't see themselves as Roman too. Certainly while villas and other architectural signs of Roman rule are uncommon in the south-west, Roman pottery and other luxury goods are recurring finds at many sites. This supports the existence of a more nuanced or layered identity, certainly by the end of Roman rule, where a Dumnonian might have thought of themselves as a Roman citizen of Dumnonian descent – or, to put it in more modern terms, a Romano-Dumnonian. Each layer in this case adds to the whole rather than completely replacing it.

A similar phenomenon can be observed in recent history with people who grew up in the British Empire. In the wake of the Second World War and the dismantling of the empire, they found themselves drawn to Britain by cultural ties as well as economic need and encouragement. They considered themselves British as well as being their own national identity. This dual identity, for good and ill, is still a major influence on the citizens of these nations today.

Returning to the tin trade, now that we have established its importance both to the local Dumnonian economy and to Europe as a whole, we must consider what this importance means for the identity and mindset of the Dumnonians. Fundamentally, we can consider that they were much more outward looking than is often assumed of Iron Age Britons. They relied on foreign trade to preserve their wealth and power and, with their position on the south-west peninsula of Britain, they were exceptionally placed to welcome that trade from the Irish Sea and Atlantic Ocean.

This is evident in the cultural similarities between the Dumnonii and the Veneti of the Armorican Peninsula (modern-day Brittany) which existed even prior to the Roman invasion [Cunliffe, 2005]. Indeed, in Caesar's Gallic Wars he used a supposed collusion between the Britons and the Veneti of Armorica as one of his motivations for an invasion of Britain.

This outward-looking focus, and the close ties to the Continent, draw our attention to one of the key facts about Dumnonia which is too often ignored in both the traditional and revisionist histories of the Early Medieval period. Instead of a kingdom suddenly cut off and alone when the Saxons took control of south-east Britain, Dumnonia was instead a country, and the Dumnonii a people, who looked westward and south to the Mediterranean at least as much as, and perhaps even more than, they looked towards their fellow Britons.

The reason this often does not bear mentioning in histories looking at the period is that it runs counter to the way we look at Britain today. To a modern mindset, London and the south-east have always been the focal point for trade and communication with the Continent. Indeed, most of our modern transport infrastructure is built to flow in exactly those directions. While this was certainly becoming the case during the years of Roman rule, when much of the imperial bureaucracy and infrastructure was built in these areas (as well as in York, or Eboracum), in the long years preceding Roman arrival and in the years following their departure, the fractious nature of Britain – a land split between many competing interests, tribal groups and warbands, both Saxon and native – meant that the Irish Sea and the Atlantic beyond were far easier trade routes to ply then attempting to move overland to the geographically closer ports around Dover and Kent.

This can be seen in the archaeology of the south-west, where it is not only Roman remains which are rare but indeed there is a large imbalance in the numbers of Bronze and Iron Age sites in Cornwall and West Devon compared to areas east of Dartmoor. The far larger number of sites, and (in general) the more impressive sites, are all in the westernmost reaches of Dumnonia, while only Exeter, as the Roman administrative capital, sees significant development during the years of imperial rule.

It's also much easier to picture if one considers the geography of the south-west peninsula during the Early Medieval period. If we consider Dumnonia to run roughly from the River Parrett in Somerset down to Cornwall, then we encounter a range of natural formations in the eastern part of the kingdom that would discourage large-scale settlement outside of Exeter.

There are, of course, first the Somerset Levels, undrained at the time and providing a formidable eastern barrier against the rest of Britain. There are also the Quantocks, which would make travel difficult, other than on the old Roman road that went between the two of these features. Moving further west, we have both Exmoor and Dartmoor, both of which would have taken up even more of the landscape then they do today and would have also been significantly less hospitable. The moorland, and the general landscape of Devon, is of course very good for farming, particularly pastoral farming and grazing, but this does not necessarily lead to a high population density.

Adding to this, we also have the large estuary of the River Exe, which was significantly more marshy and open than it appears today with modern holiday towns built to take advantage of the waterfront space. Of course, there is also an internal barrier between west Devon and modern Cornwall in the form of the Tamar and its own wide estuary and feeder rivers, recognised today as the Tamar Valley AONB. This perhaps explains why, later in the Western Kingdom's history, it became the natural border between Wessex and Cornwall.

When we look at Dumnonia in this way – outward-looking and facing, rather than insular – we can perhaps appreciate that, at least in those early years following Roman withdrawal, the most immediate concern to the ruling elite wouldn't have been events in the distant east of Britain but rather how to maintain the lucrative trade routes to the Mediterranean that brought in so much wealth.

We can see evidence of this wealth in the finds from Cornwall dated to the post-Roman period. These include the large quantities of imported Mediterranean pottery found both at Tintagel [Nowakowski and Gossip, 2017] and at the large trading settlement of Bantham, which lies on Devon's south coast, close to modern-day Plymouth. The Bantham finds are particularly significant, as the pottery assemblage represents the second-largest find of Roman amphorae in the south-west [Reed et al., 2011]. The main assemblage has also been dated to between the fifth and sixth centuries, meaning that the trade was still flourishing. Indeed, Bantham may have been at a high point in the years after the Romans left, rather than before. Earlier digs at the site found evidence of occupation into the seventh century, after which evidence became more sporadic.

Nor is the imported pottery entirely restricted to a small number of specific sites such as the royal estate at Tintagel or the trading town at Bantham. Recent digs at Mothecombe, a site a few kilometres from Bantham itself, have revealed a smaller settlement that still has occurrences of imported ware. This shows a wider distribution of the goods amongst the Dumnonian elite, as Mothecombe is assumed to be a high-status dwelling, possibly for a local representative of the king/central authority [Agate et al., 2012]. It is worth mentioning at this point that evidence for occupation at Mothecombe also ends around the end of the seventh century, very similarly to Bantham.

There have also been a number of finds in recent years around Cornwall, particularly of Early Medieval, immediately post-Roman, jewellery. These include belt buckles, a bird mount which marks an intermediary point between Roman and Anglo-Saxon styles (PAS reference CORN-4C58B4) as well as a number of strap ends. Of particular note is an animal-shaped brooch (CORN-D9B9D4) which shows similarity in the figure shape to those decorated in patterns on quoit-brooch style brooches, which are common Continental and Early Anglo-Saxon finds. However, the size of the beast is much more reminiscent of Frankish animal brooches. This suggests that either the jeweller who made the piece, or else the customer who commissioned it, was intimately familiar with a range of styles popular on the Continent and elsewhere in Britain. This reinforces a cultural viewpoint intimately tied to the rest of Early Medieval Europe.

All of this fits with the image of a trading elite who, finding their former supply networks disrupted by the removal of the Roman tax and trade structures and chaos in the east, have returned to the sea for their primary trading network. It should be made clear at this point that this would have been a pivot to existing routes, in place since antiquity, rather than a total revolution in trade. While it is very likely, given what we know about Roman Britain, that the Roman state had prioritised trade overland on the road network so that goods could be moved to the Continent via the English Channel (this also would have allowed more efficient taxation and control, and explains the presence of military encampments along the roads in the south-west), there would have always been trade via the sea lanes. Particularly as moving goods, especially large heavy items like metal ingots, is much easier to do via ship.

With this context in mind, we can then examine another key feature both of the period and central to understanding Dumnonia. It is a story which is often remarked upon but has perhaps in the past been misconstrued; specifically, the oversea movement of Britons from the south-west and Wales to Armorica, and the foundation of Brittany as well as a second, often overlooked, colony in Galicia, Spain.

The traditional narratives around the foundation of Brittany are that pressure from the Anglo-Saxons caused what was essentially a refugee movement to form, which resulted in Britons fleeing mainland Britain and heading for the Continent. However, as we have seen, the immediate chaos of the Adventus Saxonum would have had a limited impact, outside of disrupting trade routes, on the Britons of the south-west and Wales. Additionally, the cultural links between Dumnonia and Armorica were longstanding and continuous, so it is inaccurate to entirely link Brittany's foundation to the actions and movements of people in the fifth and sixth centuries. While modern scholarship does support a two-stage movement of people to the peninsula, even this is perhaps more a feature of the various British rebellions of the late Roman period and the movement of British troops from the islands onto the mainland, which provided an initial base for later colonisation efforts.

Indeed, a key element to consider when we look at narratives of refugees or forced movement is that the legacy left behind in Brittany showcases a major and long-lasting cultural shift when compared to the rest of France in this period. The Bretons, as they would become, formed a distinctive identity with their own native language that remained the culture of the ruling class into the Medieval period, while the language itself survives even today. If the settlers were simply fleeing for their safety, it is unlikely they would have been able to so completely take control of an area that, while culturally similar, was not directly under their control.

With this in mind, we can see the movements to Brittany and Galicia not as a rushed movement caused by external pressure, but instead as a deliberate undertaking by a focused and energetic elite. As for the why, this is extremely obvious to discern when we view Dumnonian interests as primarily focused on the tin trade and controlling movement of goods into the Mediterranean.

If one were to look at a geological map of Europe, specifically looking for natural deposits of tin, the obvious high concentration around Devon and Cornwall would be well known. However, there are additional deposits in Brittany and in Galicia, both of which were well known and to varying extents exploited during antiquity. By establishing colonies over or close to these deposits, the Dumnonian elite not only secured ports for the sale and shipment of tin, they also physically took control of deposits and the mining therein.

While it seems unlikely that these colonies were ever centrally governed from south-west Britain, it is very much the Dumnonian Elite who took up residence in each location and were, for a short period in Galicia but permanently in Brittany, able to exert both control and influence over local affairs. You can see the direct links most clearly in the early names of the Breton regions, specifically Domonee (Dumnonia) and Cournaille (Cerniu or Cornwall), as well as linguistically where Breton and Cornish remained mutually intelligible into the early modern period.

Such undertakings would have been extremely expensive to outfit and supply, not to mention draining on manpower, as we know that the Bretons in particular did come into conflict with their neighbours, particularly once the Frankish state was fully established later in the period. We can therefore surmise that the Dumnonian elite felt secure enough in their own position and wealth that they could afford such expense in pursuit of the greater goal of maintaining their preeminent position in the European tin trade.

This willingness to build and invest is further showcased by a number of large-scale building projects undertaken in the closing years of Roman rule and the centuries beyond. Tintagel, the great fortress of the Dumnonian royalty, was expanded and fortified during this period with a range of high-status dwellings now excavated, and evidence of ritualised feasting now well documented. Additionally, the Giant's Hedge was constructed on the northern end of the Looe Peninsula. This is a highly significant undertaking, a large defensive work that would have taken hundreds of workers and man hours to complete. On a smaller, more local scale it seems some of the 'rounds' – characteristic Cornish settlements usually consisting of several dwellings inside a raised enclosure – were also fortified in this period, including the settlement at Trethurgy. Given that Trethurgy in particular, and rounds more generally, are thought to be sites often linked with local leaders, this again reflects a native elite on the rise.

However, we must consider why so much effort was going into defensive works if Dumnonia was, as we have argued, a single and powerful unit. Certainly, it doesn't seem at this stage that civil conflict was a primary concern in the way it may have been further east. As noted, the continuity of tribal allegiance is notable in Dumnonia, and there don't seem to be large-scale signs of destruction from this period. However, we do know from folklore, supported by archaeological evidence, that there were increasing numbers of raiders and settlers coming, not from Denmark and Germany but from Ireland. This could be a contributing factor to the construction of defences; however, it would appear that the raids were sporadic and never approach the same level of threat as the later Viking raiders would pose to the established order of Europe.

Indeed, while both Cornwall and Devon contain a number of Ogham (ancient Irish script) inscribed stones, they are all bilingual, with corresponding inscriptions in Latin, and usually commemorate people with non-Irish names. This suggests that, while there were indeed incoming settlers from Ireland, they were adapting and taking on native language and habits as much as preserving their own.

We can also contrast the defensive works in Devon and Cornwall with those further afield, such as Cadbury Castle in Somerset. This former Iron Age hill fort was reoccupied in the post-Roman period by a powerful local elite (potentially a Dumnonian lord but more likely the king or ruler of another tribal kingdom) and refortified despite being several miles inland and a fair distance away from the continuing turmoil in the south-east. This would seem to suggest that, while Cadbury undoubtedly held a military significance in terms of the warriors who would have accompanied the lord, as well as its position close to the former Roman road, there were other non-military reasons for the occupation.

Similar sites in Wales can also be identified where the reason for occupation does not seem to be immediate military need. So it becomes necessary to examine non-military rationales for taking over and fortifying such sites. Perhaps the most obvious reason is to make a very powerful statement. Fortresses like Tintagel and South Cadbury Castle are very visible landmarks in the countryside, often seen from great distances away. They speak very plainly a message: 'I am here and I built this.' In a period of great uncertainty, like that which followed the Roman withdrawal, it would have been a powerful message of stability sent out by the elite to the rest of society. The Romans may be gone but we are still capable of great works. Additionally, in a warrior-dominated society as north-west Europe was in the Early Medieval period, it projects an image of strength that was inherently tied to rulership.

In addition it is important to note that several of the sites for which we have evidence of reoccupation are former Iron Age strongholds from the pre-Roman period. Many of these, particularly in the west, would have had cultural memories and traditions attached to them, a physical reminder of the non-Roman parts of local identity. By taking over and reoccupying these sites, as well as constructing new sites in similar styles, the ruling class could emphasise a sense of continuity rather than disruption, and as such reinforce their own legitimacy.

Correspondingly, the post-Roman period sees a decline in the fortunes of Isca Dumnorum (Exeter) as the business of rulership seems to have shifted naturally back west to reflect the new reality we have already discussed. It is perhaps worth considering here that the Dumnonian elite seem to make a conscious effort not to tie their rulership to the imperial order, instead opting to present themselves in a more native light. Certainly, it doesn't seem like there were pressing needs to flee the city; even today, up to 70 per cent of the Roman walls are still standing, albeit with significant repair and replacement work by following generations.

If we view it in this context, as part of a press for legitimacy by the newly independent elite, we can also begin to understand why the refortification of many sites seems so short-lived. For example, many of the Cornish rounds disappear over the fifth and sixth centuries to be replaced with more spread-out hamlets and villages bearing the place name 'Tref', from which the modern element 'Tre' descends. This has sometimes been interpreted as evidence of rapid conquest, particularly by Victorian historians and archaeologists; however, it probably reflects a settling in of the new order, with people less on edge. The down sides of a closed-in fortified settlement (not least of which would be hygiene and the marshalling of animals) may have started to outweigh the positives.

There is a final element we must consider when introducing Dumnonia at the end of the Roman period, and that is the growth of Christianity in the region. While Cornwall is often credited as the 'Land of Saints' in the Early Medieval period, it is worth examining what we know about the establishment of Christianity in the region and how this may inform our picture of the Dumnonian state.

If we look at the stories of the Cornish saints, for these are probably the stories with the most to say about Cornwall in the Early Medieval period, we are given tales of superheroic feats undertaken by missionaries from Ireland and Wales against a land still replete with pagan chieftains and angry monsters. However, aside from the normal supernatural elements one expects with Medieval hagiography of this type, there is also an underlying sense of 'otherness' to the stories. This is perhaps explained by many of them coming to us not from Cornish or Welsh sources, but from documents recorded in England in the thirteenth and fourteenth centuries.

This includes the patron saint of Cornwall, Saint Piran, whose only surviving *Vita* exists in a compendium of West Country saints held in the Gotha Ducal archives in Germany. It was produced in Devon, possibly in Tavistock, around the fourteenth century. It's notable that much of this *Vita* is actually that of an Irish saint, Ciaran, with events in Cornwall then tacked on to the end. It's also worth noting that the date places the production of the *Vita* around the time that Devon's Stannary Parliament was being created, which may explain the odd story of Piran 'rediscovering' tin mining which, as we have noted, was the major trading concern of the south-west Britons from the Bronze Age right through Roman rule and beyond. Potentially in this case the forces behind the Stannary push wished to give their profession a heavenly patron.

Despite issues of veracity in content, the saint stories do have some corroboration in fact and local folklore. For example, there is indeed an Early Medieval chapel amongst the sands at Piran Sands, near Perranporth (Piran's Port), supporting the tradition of his landing there. There are actually two churches as Piran's Old Church, the church built in the tenth century after the original small oratory was overwhelmed by the dunes, was itself overwhelmed and buried (both have now been excavated and can be viewed).

Similarly, there is a large corpus of early Christian stonework throughout Cornwall and Devon, including the Ogham inscriptions already mentioned. The majority of this stonework shows classic patterns of the Insular style, said to originate in Ireland but certainly appearing commonly in Ireland, Wales, Cornwall and Brittany. Additionally, the place name 'Lan' (e.g. Lanhydrock) is relatively common throughout Cornwall, occurring more than fifty times with a religious connotation of some form. This usually takes the form of a dedication to a saint, as is the case in Lanhydrock (St Hydrock being another of the semi-mythical saints). Though technically 'Lan' merely defines an enclosure of land, it is fairly commonly associated with religious sites, and in particular Early Medieval religious sites, in Cornwall and in Brittany (e.g. Landevennec).

So we can say with some certainty that the early Church was very active, potentially with a large number of missionaries from Ireland spreading its message, the memory of whom eventually would give rise to the bombastic saints' tales that are such a feature of local folklore. This then begs the question: why are there so many in Dumnonia?

It does not appear, so far as we can tell, that the south-west was a particular hotbed of paganism in the post-Roman period, although it can be very difficult to understand what faiths, if any, were vying with Christianity in the post-Roman landscape. The empire had only made Christianity its official religion in 380, uncomfortably close to the earliest dates for Roman rule to end in Britain. With that being said, it had been legalised since 313, and we know that there certainly were Christians in Roman Britain. When we think back to St Germanus and his missions to Britain, it becomes clear that there was some kind of organised Church in place in Britain at that time (albeit one which was at risk of Pelagianism) with at least loose ties to the Church on the Continent.

It seems reasonable to assume that Dumnonia, being an outward-looking and trading kingdom, would also have a significant Christian presence already within it. Additionally, if it did not, we would perhaps expect Gildas to be more damning in his writings, albeit that he wrote much later in the period.

So if it is not just the business of saving souls that brings Irish missionaries to Dumnonia, what does?

First of all, we may consider the presence of Irish missionaries to be indicative of the importance, which we've already discussed, of the Irish Sea and Atlantic as major trade routes. Similar finds and stories of saints are also common in Wales, showing that the missionaries were indeed using the Irish Sea as an expedient network to spread their message. Again, this runs counter to some of our presumptions about the importance of the Channel or south-east Britain to Britons living in the west.

Viewing the large missionary presence in the context we've developed for Dumnonia – rich, outward-looking and relatively stable – it could well be that there was a political element to the conversion. The Irish Church was, after all, different from the central Church on the Continent which was slowly starting to develop a stricter hierarchy and practices, all of which tied back to the Pope. The Irish Church meanwhile looked towards Iona and the great monastery there rather than to Rome.

This conflict would eventually come to a head at the Synod of Whitby but, given what we know of Church relations, would have been growing more obvious for decades leading up to that point. By investing resources into converting Dumnonia and the Welsh kingdoms, the Irish Church, although it wasn't quite so well organised as its title suggests, was perhaps securing for itself a power base outside of Ireland and the Scottish Isles. Certainly, Tintagel eventually was home to a group of educated scribes as previously mentioned. These were most likely monks or otherwise involved in religious life, placing a core of faithful right at the heart of Dumnonian power.

Having thus introduced Dumnonia at the end of Roman rule, we now need to turn to the other major player in the Early Medieval history of the south-west: the Anglo-Saxon kingdom of Wessex.

3

WESSEX: FINDING A PLACE IN THE HEPTARCHY

Wessex occupies a singular place in British history. After all, it is from Wessex that Alfred and his heirs will one day forge England. It is perhaps no surprise, then, that much of the scholarship around Wessex focuses on those later monarchs and the conflicts with the Vikings in the ninth and tenth centuries. A drawback of this approach is that it lends an air of assumed superiority to Wessex. Surely, as the only Anglo-Saxon kingdom to weather the Viking storm intact, it must always have been destined for greatness?

This assumption does a great disservice to a number of great rulers, only one of whom we today call 'The Great', who took a disparate collection of small warbands and polities and managed to eventually form a cohesive whole from them. Because at the time of Wessex's founding, the kingdom's survival, let alone its success, was not a given.

Differing accounts are given as to the founding of Wessex. The *Anglo-Saxon Chronicle* states that Cerdic and Cynric arrived around 495 and immediately made war upon the Welsh, 'first gaining the lands of Wessex' [Avalon, 2008]. The *Chronicle* then goes on to discuss their nephews Stuf and Wihtgar arriving in the same area and conquering much of modern-day Hampshire and the Isle of Wight. The conflation of these two narratives is often given as the origins of Wessex.

However, the Venerable Bede, in his *Historia ecclesiastica gentis Anglorum*, puts ownership of the Isle of Wight and Hampshire in the hands of Jutes, not Saxons. He further states that the West Saxons were known as the Gewisse and then describes how they eventually came and slaughtered the inhabitants of the Isle of Wight in 685.

The image this conflation of origins seems to paint is one of a smaller group, or a series of smaller groups, all fighting amongst themselves for a foothold in southern Britain. The historical record seems to agree with the *Chronicle* that the focus of these activities was around the Thames Valley. This has recently been supported by the excavation of a high-status warrior burial at a hilltop near Marlow, overlooking the Thames Valley. The burial included a sword and spears, as well as a number of high-status goods. This adds to an extensive concentration of high-status Anglo-Saxon goods in the Upper Thames Valley [Hamerow et al., 2013], further building the picture of a concentrated growth in Germanic settlers in the region, although to which tribe they would affiliate themselves is obviously a tricky question to answer in practice.

While the exact origins of Wessex in this period are difficult to discern, it does seem that warfare was a relatively common refrain, with mentions in the *Chronicle* of the fighting already mentioned around the Isle of Wight, but also further east with the men of Kent as well as with a number of other minor polities. It's worth noting that this is, in fact, the first mention in the *Chronicle* of fighting between different Germanic groups. This may suggest that the conditions which allowed for potentially peaceful migration – the breakdown of Roman stability, the loss of identity without strong regional ties to fall back on, and potentially the deprivations of petty warlords – had decreased or perhaps disappeared altogether. This would make for a more hazardous environment for the new tribal group to emerge into, one where they are immediately put under pressure by other groups and newly established kingdoms of their fellow Anglo-Saxons. This is a pattern which is to colour much of the history of Wessex and, crucially for our purposes, their relationship with the Britons to their west.

Another interesting feature of this early Wessex is that many of its rulers, including the perhaps semi-mythological Cerdic and Cynric, have names either wholly Brythonic in origin or incorporating Briton elements with Saxon elements. This has sometimes been interpreted as the survival of a Briton polity which merged with an emerging Saxon one; however, the material expression of culture appears to be wholly Germanic in practice. Additionally, we would expect later writers with an already dim view of Wessex – such as Bede, who was an ardent Northumbrian – to use such origins against them in their writings. As it is, it seems to go without mention.

Alternatively, it may be that the incoming settlers intermarried with native elites, and the subsequent namings reflect this co-mingling. Of course, this sort of mixing would support some of the more peaceful transition models of the Anglo-Saxon migrations which have become more standard in modern thinking.

The final option may simply be an attempt to assume the trappings of traditional power or leadership in the region by taking the names and/or titles of the previous rulers. This could be seen as a distant echo of the process under way on the Continent where the emerging Frankish kingdom took on more visible symbolism of the former Roman state and absorbed the existing elites (as well as their knowledge and some of the infrastructure they held key roles within) [Dodd, 2016].

Of course, as we have already frequently commented, ideas of identity and nationality are extremely tricky to interpret in the past. More than that, sometimes things we take as solid signifiers of these facets would have been unremarkable in the period. This may be the more likely explanation for the Brythonic names in Wessex's regnal lists.

Regardless, the pattern of small-scale combat appears to be the norm until Ceawlin, another Briton-named king and potentially Cerdic's grandson, enters the *Chronicle* in the late sixth century. Initially he is mentioned beside his father in 556, fighting against an unknown group of Britons at the place called Beran Byrg, or Beran's Fortress. This is sometimes identified as Barbury Castle in Wiltshire, although the *Chronicle* is typically short of details that could make this certain. Given the situation in Britain by the late sixth century, though, it does seem that a site west of the Thames Valley would be most likely; as we have discussed, most of the real estate to the south and east was by this time firmly in the control of Anglo-Saxons.

The *Chronicle* doesn't specify who was victorious; however, given Ceawlin's later career it is perhaps tempting to identify this as a pivotal moment for him. Confronted by more firmly established kingdoms all around his own, he could perhaps see the potential that the more fractured situation amongst the Briton tribes provided. Ceawlin would become king in 560 or thereabouts (the regnal lists, Bede and the different versions of the *Chronicle* all disagree) but we know very little of his actions until 568, when he and his brother Cutha fight King Aethelbert of Kent and put him to flight. This victory is notable as Athelbert is, in most sources, a highly regarded king in his own right. His status is aided in this by being, according to Bede, the first English ruler to convert to Christianity, and by his close relationship with the Frankish court. Bede further lists him as the third of his 'Bretwala' or over-rulers of the English kings.

Ceawlin is himself recorded by Bede as one of these rulers, and this combined with his recorded defeat of Athelbert tells us something about the victorious career he must have had. After all, Ceawlin was by all accounts an avowed pagan. Had there been an opportunity to diminish his achievements, Bede, and the Christian writers of the *Chronicle*, likely would have taken it.

As it is, Ceawlin is on the offensive again extremely quickly. In 571 he and another figure, Cuthwine (potentially this is an alternative translation of Cutha), are fighting the Britons at a place called Biedcanforda, taking control of four towns: Bensingtun (Benson, Oxfordshire), Egonesham (Eynsham, Oxfordshire), Liggeeanburh (Limbury, Bedfordshire) and Aeglesburh (Aylesbury, Buckinghamshire) [Thorpe, 1861]. This battle is controversial for many historians, including J.N.L. Myres [1986] and Frank Stenton [2001]; however, what is important for our discussion is the tradition it began of listing, in the *Chronicle*, specific towns taken during a Saxon victory.

Additionally, it firmly establishes Ceawlin's priorities to be westward. In the light of the recent victory over Athelbert this may seem unusual; we would perhaps expect an effort to capitalise on the initial victory. However, given Bede's commentary and Athelbert's own well-documented rule, Ceawlin may have been aware of a long-term weakness in his position compared to the Kentish kings, probably at least partly stemming from the continental links that the latter enjoyed which are not as evident in the archaeological record for Wessex.

Regardless of motivation, he continued pushing westward aggressively, facing a coalition of British kings at Deorham. This battle is often overlooked, or its importance minimised to the geographical and linguistic changes it would force onto the Britons; however, the stakes for Ceawlin and Wessex are absolutely worth considering. As mentioned, while he had defeated Athelbert once it was by no means certain that he and his forces would repeat that victory in a subsequent confrontation. Equally, the forces of three separate British tribes would have been a significant threat, each one able to maintain its own independence in the face of Saxon expansion for over a century by that point. If they had been able to defeat Ceawlin and his forces it is entirely possible that Wessex would never have solidified into an important part of the Heptarchy, and instead may have gone the way of other minor kingdoms such as Essex or Sussex; a regional power that is eventually absorbed by a larger neighbour.

It is perhaps worth noting that the names of the three British kings opposing Ceawlin – Conmail, Condidan and Farinmail – are all archaic in format. This suggests that the scribes working on the *Chronicle* perhaps had access to an older written or oral source, perhaps denoting a larger importance once placed on the battle in local, West Saxon sources.

All the sources do agree that Ceawlin is the victor in this battle and, according to the *Chronicle*, he seized control of Gloucester, Cirencester and Bath. While translations may sometimes be questioned, all of these had been Roman

towns, not quite on the level of London perhaps but still regionally important (Bath in particular had once held significant religious attachments). The
matched number of kings to towns, and their importance, potentially suggests
that these were the power centres of the British groups. This is significant
because all three sites were essentially Roman constructions. Gloucester and
Cirencester both started life as legionary fortresses before civil towns expanded
around them, while the waters at Bath, or Aquae Sullis to the Romans, had
held religious importance in pre-Roman Britain – it was the Romans who
had built up the town and the elaborate baths around it. This means that the
Britons had constructed new identities for themselves based on highly localised concerns, rather than an overarching tribal identity as may have been the
case further west.

This perhaps meant that, despite the attempt to work together against
Ceawlin, the British kings were still riven with their own disagreements and
histories, which may have assisted their defeat. It also shows the extent to
which high levels of Romanisation were perhaps detrimental to the survival of
Romano-British identities during the migration period. However, we should
also be conscious not to ascribe too much success to other groups purely on
the basis of identity or culture. As we can see with Ceawlin and will see with
other leaders, opportunities must be exploited by groups in order to succeed.

The fallout of the victory was monumental. Firstly, and most often identified,
the victory at Deorham meant that an Anglo-Saxon group had reached the
Severn Estuary and effectively cut off overland communication between the
south-west Britons and those who lived in Wales or the Old North. Generally,
linguists use this date as a starting point for the divergence between Welsh,
Cumbric and Cornish languages (Breton remains closely linked to Cornish,
diverging at a slightly later date). However, it should be noted that, while certain
Welsh kings claimed to have been ruler of Britain during this period, overall
levels of cooperation between the Britons seem to have remained extremely
low. As such, this may not have been the sort of hugely significant cultural shift
we imagine. As we have already seen, it is possible Dumnonia wass much more
focused on the Irish Sea and beyond than it is events on the land.

It does, however, seem extremely unlikely that the rulers of Dumnonia,
intimately concerned with trade as we have seen, would be unaware of these
new developments despite their potential distance and isolation from them.

Of more immediate note, at least militarily, is that both Cirencester and
Gloucester sit astride the Fosse Way, one of the great Roman roads linking
Isca Dumnorum (Exeter) to Lincoln. Additionally, Cirencester acted as a
junction between this and the Akerman Way, which itself linked to Watling

Street. This means that not only had Wessex physically driven a wedge between Wales and the south-west, but also that it was able to control trade on the road. This would have secured a valuable revenue stream for the West Saxons, as well as providing obvious logistical benefits for moving and sup-plying their own forces.

Thus Wessex had secured itself breathing space, as well as significant land and resources. While still not the most powerful of the Saxon kingdoms, it was now a force to be reckoned with rather than ignored or absorbed. Thus victory at Deorham could be argued as the foundational moment of Wessex itself; the point where the small tribal collection of warriors and war leaders became a proper political power. Ceawlin had also begun the slow westward expansion which would come to define much of Wessex's history in the pre-Viking age. This was to be a tactic he and his successors would revisit, often when under pressure from their fellow Saxons, and it would inevitably lead to conflict with Dumnonia when their borders eventually came into contact.

4

AN INTRODUCTION TO EARLY MEDIEVAL WARFARE

We have now set the scene and introduced both Dumnonia and the emerging power of Wessex that would eventually challenge it. In the next section we will, by the nature of events, be discussing military confrontations between both sides. As such, it seems an opportune moment to discuss some of what is known about weapons and warfare in this period.

This is particularly important when it comes to the Britons of Dumnonia, as there are many misconceptions about the way in which the Brythonic peoples fought which are worth discussing and dismissing before we discuss the battles themselves.

To begin with, we should acknowledge that it is difficult to discuss Early Medieval warfare as a single unified whole. After all, the period runs from 500 until 1066 and this is a very long time for anything to remain stagnant [Underwood, 1999]. For the Saxons, the period marks a change from small warbands gathered around Lords, Chieftains and Kings, to a more professionalised military elite and their retainers, spanning not just the top 1 per cent of society but also those in the Thegnly class (that is, landholders who owe military service) who might be considered to be the upper middle classes by our modern terminology.

However, there are some consistent themes that bridge both time and cultures which we should bear in mind while considering military confrontations between Wessex and Dumnonia.

The most basic building block of any Early Medieval army starts with the retainers or companions of the army leader. Kings and wealthy lords would gather around themselves groups of elite warriors whom they would outfit, feed and provide shelter to in return for service in battle (as well as the collection of taxes and other services best conducted by armed men). When the king called he would further expect his lords or chieftains to bring their own retainers with them, thus building up a core of experienced and well-equipped fighters for the army.

For the Saxons, these were the Hearth-Guard (eventually Huscarls or House-Carls following Danish influence), while Dumnonian lords would refer to the Teylu or 'Family'. In either society the role was the same.

Military service, as well as the bonds of companionship it helped form, was one of the basic building blocks of Early Medieval society. Failing to do your duty to the king or your lord was seen as an incredibly serious failing. So much so that the Laws of King Ine (who we'll meet later) set out the penalties as follows:

> If a nobleman who holds land neglects military service, he shall pay 120 shillings and forfeit his land; a nobleman who holds no land shall pay 60 shillings; a commoner shall pay a fine of 30 shillings for neglecting military service.

The loss of land in particular would have been an enormous blow for a lord in a society as heavily dependent on agriculture as Early Medieval Britain was.

Further, the reciprocal bonds of lordship meant that military service didn't stop at providing and equipping armed men (certainly in the early period) – you were also expected to lead from the front, in the shield wall and often in the thickest of the fighting. To do less while asking your companions to take the risks on your behalf would be seen as a failing by the lord.

Beyond the professional warriors, Early Medieval rulers could also call upon freemen to bear arms as part of an army. Perhaps the best known of these is the Saxon fyrd, but equally the Brythonic lords could call upon the Llu or army. In either case the service was only temporary, usually lasting no more than a matter of weeks in order not to disrupt the cycles of agricultural life.

While the popular image of these armies is a mass of poorly equipped peasants, this owes more to fantasy than it does reality. Given the importance of warfare to elite status in the Early Medieval world, it is perhaps unsurprising that war was treated as a serious business. Commoners called to serve in the Fyrd or Llu were often doing so not just out of obligation but for the chance to better their own positions, either through glory, renown or plunder. They were also expected to arrive fully armed at their own expense, usually meaning bearing a shield with a metal boss and at least a spear to fight with although this varied widely within the period. By the end of Anglo-Saxon Britain the armaments of a Fyrdman included horses, armour and weapons. As such, while not at the same level as the professional warriors, a king could expect these fighters to at least have put some time into training in the use of their own weapons and, in the case of long campaigns or wars, they may have some experience of fighting already.

Most fighting at the start of the period was likely quite open, taking the form of small-scale raiding and clashes between smaller bands of warriors, but eventually larger-scale conflicts often resolved in the clash of shield walls – lines of men whose shields overlapped one another in order to make a solid defensive wall to fight behind. This is a nasty and extremely brutal form of warfare as you are pressed forward until you are face to face with your foe. It is perhaps little wonder that many conflicts and battles ended not with a stand-up fight but with one side breaking and fleeing.

In comparison to their Saxon neighbours, and even the foreign Vikings who arrived on the British Isles during our period, the Brythonic people of Wales, Cumbria and Cornwall are poorly represented in academic works and discussion of military history. While finding a list of battles, and even some of their locations, can be relatively straightforward, the details of how the Britons fought are much harder to piece together.

This means that for a long time historians and re-enactors have had to rely on sources from outside the Early Medieval period in an attempt to glean an insight into the workings of Brythonic armies between 500 and 1066. Unfortunately, this means that some sources have been accepted uncritically when perhaps they deserved more interrogation.

The clearest example of this can be found in the popular view of Welsh, and by extension Brythonic, warfare. There is a very strong and persistent image of the British warrior as a lightly armed skirmisher; a fighter relying on hit-and-run or guerrilla tactics in the face of stronger or better-armed opponents. This image is strongly ingrained in many circles and is sometimes embraced as a source of pride.

Whatever truth there may be to this view, much of the evidence comes not from our period but from the years following 1066 when the Normans, leading a unified 'English' army, invaded Wales and attempted to subdue it to the English crown.

While in this instance the Welsh princes were very much outnumbered by their Norman opponents, and in some ways outmatched, even here we should wonder aloud about the view of almost 'primitive' Welshmen fighting a more powerful foe. Much of it can be traced back to the writings of Gerald of Wales, a twelfth-century chronicler. As Gerald wrote: 'This people is light and active, hardy rather than strong.'

He spoke of Welsh courage, of unarmed men fighting against cavalry but, in the same text, he wrote:

In war this nation is very severe in the first attack, terrible by their clamour and looks, filling the air with horrid shouts and the deep-toned clangour of very long trumpets; swift and rapid in their advances and frequent throwing of darts. Bold in the first onset, they cannot bear a repulse, being easily thrown into confusion as soon as they turn their backs; and they trust to flight for safety, without attempting to rally, which the poet thought reprehensible in martial conflicts.

As Gerald is one of the few sources talking about Anglo-Norman and Welsh relations, his descriptions are often used as a primary source and then applied uncritically across history.

However, it's worth remembering that Gerald (despite his name) was as much English as he was Welsh, even serving in the court of Henry II. He was also writing primarily for an Anglo-Norman audience and took pains in his prose to paint the Welsh as exotic outsiders at best, and downright primitive savages at worst.

This is particularly egregious in situations, as Davies [2014] points out, where Gerald describes the same set of ambush or feigned retreat tactics used by a Norman lord as 'ingenious' or sound tactics, while simultaneously condemning the Welsh for their use.

So if this image may not be the most accurate, is there anything we can pull from the sources about Brythonic warfare in the Early Medieval period?

While cattle-raiding and other 'irregular warfare' was common to all the people of the British Isles, when it came to actual warfare between bands of trained fighters then shield walls and other unit tactics were fairly ubiquitous.

This is perhaps most clearly illustrated at the start of the period, when the memories of professional Roman armies would still be fresh amongst the elite. In the late fifth or early sixth century an illustrated copy of Virgil's *Aeneid* was produced. While the copy we have now rests in the Vatican library (Catalogue Number Vat.Lat.3867) the site of its production has been argued by Ken Dark and others to be somewhere in western Britain, potentially in Somerset. This obviously puts it potentially right at the borderlands of Dumnonia.

Among the many images in the manuscript there is a full battle scene between two armies; each of them has lined up in shieldwall to face the other and, while there are some fantastical touches such as the plumed helmets of the combatants, it seems otherwise a fairly grounded illustration as though this was something the artist was intimately familiar with.

Nor is this the only hint that shieldwall combat was relatively commonplace among the Britons. In *Y Gododdin*, a Welsh poem commemorating a battle with the Saxons of Deira, the following stanza commemorates one of the fighters:

A man went to Catraeth with the dawn,
About him a fort, a fence of shields.
Harshly they attacked, gathered booty,
Loud like thunder the noise of the shields.
A proud man, a wise man, a strong man,
He fought and pierced with spears,
Above the blood, he slew with swords.
In the strife, with hard weapons on heads.
In the court the warrior was humble,
Before Erthgi great armies would groan.

A clear reference to fighting in a shieldwall.

It may be that the Welsh and Cornish made more use of horses in battle than the Saxons or Vikings did, although all three did in fact use cavalry in some way (just not the heavy cavalry of the later Norman knight).

In both *Y Gododdin* and *Geraint ab Erbin* (*Geraint, son of Erbin*) (a poem potentially commemorating King Geraint of Dummonia's death at Llongborth) the references to horses are frequent:

Before Geraint, the unflinching foe,
I saw horses jaded and gory from the battle,
And after the shout, a terrible impulsion.

In Anglo-Saxon sources, such as the Battle of Maldon, on the other hand, the mentions of horses tend to be briefer, usually involving riding to the location of the battle and then sending them away:

Then he ordered each of his warriors his horse to loose
Far off to send it and forth to go,
To be mindful of his hands and of his high heart.
Then did Offa's Kinsman first know
That the earl would not brook cowardice.

It also was not unusual for raiding Vikings to seek tribute in horses in order to improve their speed and mobility away from their ships. Both Saxons and Vikings would use cavalry when appropriate, such as when hunting for a broken foe.

Where the difference becomes clear is in the treatment of the horse and cavalry in heroic poetry, where it forms a much more central platform in Old Welsh sources than in any comparable Saxon tale or Viking saga.

Returning to *Y Goddodin*, the warriors it commemorates are most often mounted and all are described as riding to the site of the battle itself:

Three hundred gold-torqued,
warlike, wonderful [...]
Three hundred proud ones,
Together, armed;
Three hundred fierce horses
Carried them forward,
Three hounds and three hundred,
Sad, they did not return.

And *Geraint ab Erbin*, the elegy for King Geraint of Dumnonia, uses horses in each of its refrains.

Similar themes are common in Welsh heroic literature, whether it is the riders pursuing the mythic boar Twrch Twyth or Culhwch riding upon his war steed to see his cousin Arthur.

These themes build an image of the high status the Britons attached to mounted combat. It seems clear that, to Brythonic people, the horse was as essential a part of the warrior's gear as his mail shirt or the fast-flashing sword.

But, given what we have briefly outlined of Early Medieval warfare, what would such mounted combat look like?

It would be very different from the heavily armoured Norman knights of 1066 and later. Not only were native horses comparatively small (most likely something akin to a Welsh mountain pony of modern breeds) but stirrups, necessary for the great lance-led charge of the knight, only became common towards the end of the Early Medieval period.

Rather than try to break an enemy line with sheer brute force, in the way the Norman charge was designed, it would seem Brythonic warriors were more likely to harass their opponents with feints and false charges, peppering their lines with thrown javelins as they did so. When the enemy formation was overextended or run ragged it would be the time to press an attack, either with infantry or with the cavalry turning around and charging.

Such tactics were common in the Roman era, where auxiliary cavalry and mounted archers would perform those tasks, and it's likely this had at least some influence on the descendants of the Romano-Britons in Dumnonia.

However, it's interesting that there are also similarities to the tactics that Caesar found when he first ventured into Britain nearly 1,000 years before, albeit with chariots rather than cavalry:

> Their mode of fighting with their chariots is this: firstly, they drive about in all directions and throw their weapons and generally break the ranks of the enemy with the very dread of their horses and the noise of their wheels; and when they have worked themselves in between the troops of horse, leap from their chariots and engage on foot.

Of course, the final charge could be dangerous. Most horses will not eagerly run into a press of men brandishing weapons, and it's perhaps worth noting that both the men of Goddodin and Geraint lost their battles.

However, when it worked well it could be a very effective tactic. Perhaps the best example of this is in the wars of the Bretons, Dumnonia's cousins across the Channel, as first Nominoe and then his son, Erispoe, asserted their independence from the Carolingian Franks.

At the Battle of Jengland (851), Erispoe's forces first harassed the Saxons whom Charles the Bald had arranged to screen his forces until they retreated behind the Franks, and then continued to harass and disrupt the Frankish forces for two days, inflicting heavy losses. Eventually the situation grew so dire that Charles himself withdrew in the dead of night, his flight caused panic to grip his forces, and with their cohesion gone the Bretons were able to slaughter many before they could retreat from the field.

It seems likely that the Bretons may have carried over their style of warfare from their once-native Dumnonia.

Whatever the specifics of the tactics, it is clear throughout the *Anglo-Saxon Chronicle* that native British forces are in fact able to meet Saxon armies in battle and, at times, defeat them.

Even as late as 1055 the Welsh were able to inflict defeat upon a united England as the sacking of Hereford showed, here recorded in the *Anglo-Saxon Chronicle*:

> And they gathered a great force with the Irishmen and the Welsh: and Earl Ralph collected a great army against them at the town of Hereford; where they met; but ere there was a spear thrown the English people fled, because they were on horses.
>
> The enemy then made a great slaughter there – about four hundred or five hundred men; they on the other side none. They went then to the

town, and burned it utterly; and the large minster also which the worthy Bishop Athelstan had caused to be built, that they plundered and bereft of relic and of reef, and of all things whatever; and the people they slew, and led some away.

As we stated earlier, sources and finds for Wales, Cornwall and the Old North are harder to come by than for the Saxon and Viking worlds around them, but as we get to grips with the subject more and more, it seems clear that some older assumptions about Brythonic warfare should be abandoned.

With this in mind, we can now return to the looming clashes between Dumnonia and Wessex with a clearer picture of just how determined and desperate these battles may have been.

PART 2

CONFLICT AND ADAPTATION: CORNWALL AND WESSEX

5

THE ARRIVAL OF WESSEX

By the late sixth century we have seen that Wessex was established as a growing regional power in southern Britain, with ambitions to continue expanding westward from the Severn Estuary region it had recently annexed. Dumnonia for its part was undergoing its own changes. The enclosed courtyard settlements were largely being reworked into more open-form farms and villages. Most of these now bore the place name 'Tref', which would eventually alter to Tre and remain present to this day (Trewhiddle, Tregony, etc.). Bernard Deacon [2016] identifies this change, and the decline of regional power centres like Tintagel and Bantham which also occurred over the next century, as the start of a sort of non-authoritarian power-sharing government.

However, as we will eventually see there was still a localised elite in place, including some form of ruling dynasty. Additionally, excavations at both Gwithian [Quinnell et al., 2007] and Duckpool/Morwenstow [Taylor, 2017] reveal industrial activities and some high-status activities as well. For example, the residents at Duckpool seem to have been involved in the extraction of dye from dog whelks. This would have produced a rich, deep purple colour extremely similar to the famous Tyrian purple of the Byzantine imperial court [Biggam 2006]. While the number of shells recovered is too small for wholesale garment dyeing, it could well have been used to produce decorative threads or small fabric strips, all of which would have been enormously valuable commodities in their own right.

This evidence seems to suggest that Dumnonia remained at least relatively wealthy and prosperous, although it is difficult to know how events like the Plague of Justinian in 541 would have impacted the region, particularly given the well-established trade links with the Mediterranean already discussed.

What is less clear is the state of Dumnonia's immediate neighbours, the Durotriges. There are signs of post-Roman activity at Cadbury Castle as we have already mentioned; however, given its location at the western end of Somerset it is entirely possible this is a Dumnonian site, although the balance of probability would seem to suggest a Durotrigan builder. Regardless of the occupant, use of the site seems to end around the close of the sixth century.

Recent excavations by the Durotriges Project from the University of Bournemouth has shed some interesting light on day-to-day life in Durotrigan territory, including a Roman villa that appears to have been abandoned and surrounded by timber structures prior to the end of Roman Britain [Russell et al., 2015]. This may suggest that there was already a turn towards tribal identity over Roman even before the official abandonment of the empire. This would somewhat fit with the chaotic image of the Western Empire and the many revolts in Britain occurring during the fourth century.

However, the Durotriges are noticeably absent in the documentary record, with no mention of kings or other elite figures and little evidence for economic activity outside the handful of sites already excavated.

The reason we should consider the state of the Durotriges at this point is that, if we assume (like Dumnonia) that they had resumed a tribal territory similar to that of the pre-Roman landscape, they would now find the aggressively expanding Wessex on their border.

In fact, it was in 584 that Ceawlin continued his westward march and met the Britons at a place called Fethanleag. According to the *Anglo-Saxon Chronicle*: 'This year Ceawlin and Cutha fought against the Britons at the place which is called Fethan-leag, and there was Cutha slain; and Ceawlin took many towns, and spoils innumerable; and wrathful he thence returned to his own.'

Traditionally this has often been recorded as a Saxon victory, usually by citing the taking of towns and spoils. However, when we compare this entry to the previous victory at Deorham, the *Chronicle* is uncharacteristically coy about what towns these were, or indeed about who, if anyone, Ceawlin had defeated.

Instead there are two inclusions which seem highly significant. In the first instance there is the death of Cutha, Ceawlin's brother. We have seen that in previous victories Ceawlin had won, Cutha (particularly if we equate him with the otherwise unknown Cuthwine) was a constant fixture at his side. Without knowledge of Ceawlin having any sons, it is even possible that Cutha was the Atheling, or next in line to the throne. His loss would have been a significant blow to Ceawlin and his ambitions for the still fledgling Wessex.

Cutha's death may also tell us something about how the battle itself went. We would probably expect Cutha to be in the main body of the Saxon forces, surrounded by his own retainers and the best of the, by now quite experienced, soldiers drawn up for the campaign. If he was slain in such an environment it perhaps paints a picture of an incredibly-hard fought battle between comparably sized and skilled forces.

Additionally there is the closing line, about wrathfully returning to his own. While this can be translated in different ways, the common thread is that Ceawlin seems to have retreated back into his own territory. This seems a strange thing for a previously expansionist leader to do in the wake of a victory.

When analysed in this way, the chances that Fethanleag was a compelling Saxon victory as at Deorham seem remote. Instead, it appears that Ceawlin and his forces met a unified force that could rival their own and, after a fierce battle, were pushed back into their previously conquered territory. Potentially this battle may have occurred at the end of a period of raiding by the Saxon forces, explaining the mention of booty and conquest, if indeed there is any truth to it beyond face-saving on the part of the chroniclers.

The site of the battle is uncertain; many of the battles in the *Chronicle* use place names that were current at the time of writing (not always the same as the events themselves) but which have been superseded. This is particularly noticeable in the south-west, where a large number of Brythonic place names are mentioned or used that have disappeared into English or Norman-French names over time.

Two popular suggestions are Fretherne in Gloucestershire, obviously largely stemming from the similarity in naming, and Stoke Lyne in Oxfordshire. There are, however, obvious problems with both of these sites.

To eliminate the least likely first: Stoke Lyne is extremely far north and east when we consider that the overall push seems to have been westwards. Further, it's entirely possible that it was already part of the Wessex heartland even before the battle of Deorham, but almost certainly was afterwards. The main point in its favour is a twelfth-century document recording a wood called 'Fethealee' in the town [Ellis, 1994]. However, this seems a thin justification given the other factors mentioned, particularly as this may just be a portmanteau of two Old English words 'Firth' and 'Lea', which would be something akin to a clearing within the woodland. ('Firth' is usually a suffix so this is not a perfect explanation; however, the link with woodlands makes it a compelling one.)

Fretherne seems to have a better claim in this context then, as it is west of Wessex's traditional heartlands in the Thames Valley and the name obviously retains some similarities. However, Fretherne is perched on the southern side of the Severn Estuary right at the mouth of the Bristol Channel. It is close to due north of Bath, which was one of the towns seized after Deorham.

Given the importance usually attached to Deorham for severing the Britons of the south-west from their cousins elsewhere, it seems unusual for Ceawlin to have to move against a location so close to that border. It would also have made his border with the Britons into an unusual salient, which seems unlikely given the scope of victory at Deorham.

It is of course possible that, if the battle did occur at Fretherne, then it reveals an interesting alternative to the traditional interpretation – specifically, that this may represent a counter-attack by the Britons which pushed back into land seized by Wessex. However, given the lack of supporting information beyond the naming similarity it is perhaps safer to accept the simpler explanation that neither of these sites represents the actual location of Fethanleag.

In order to better site the battle, we have to consider the position of Wessex and Ceawlin following his victory at Deorham. As previously noted, the seizing of Bath and the other cities meant he now effectively controlled large stretches of the former Roman road network, including sections of the Fosse Way which led westward towards Exeter.

Roman roads were vitally important for the movement of goods and people long after the Romans left, with much of our modern road network still incorporating sections of these ancient trackways. Roads also served a distinctly military purpose: an army attempting to move cross-country would make slow progress and risked being separated or surprised by their opponents, while moving over the wide Roman roads (originally built by the legions for this express purpose) would be safer and logistically much easier.

The importance of the road to the Saxon military mind can be seen later in the period with the construction and maintenance of Herepaths, literally 'army (Here) roads', becoming of increasing importance from the reign of Alfred the Great onwards [Gelling, 1993]. So it seems logical that Ceawlin, invested in expanding his kingdom westward as we have already seen, would use the Fosse Way from Bath to move his army and attempt to bring the Britons to battle as he had done at Deorham.

Following the route of the Roman road towards Ilchester, there are no obvious place names to match with Fethanleag, but, as we have discussed, this is often the case when relying purely on place-name evidence. It is instead prudent to consider the problem from the perspective of Ceawlin's opponents. They have a hostile army moving overland into their territory, likely focused on the Roman road but ranging from it to do some pillaging and raiding along the way. In order to stop them you need to face them in battle, ideally at a place of your choosing, where you have the advantage but they need to engage with you to advance.

As it happens, there is an ideal site around 16 miles from Bath just outside the modern town of Shepton Mallet. At a place called Beacon Hill, the Fosse Way climbs steeply up a slope and cuts through a series of ancient barrow mounds surrounded by an earth bank enclosure. Why the Romans would go to such trouble to build their road through the burial site is unknown, though it strongly suggests the site at one point held either political or religious significance to the Durotriges and the Romans wanted to make some kind of point.

The hill today is also surrounded by woodland, as the land was never enclosed, and it is easy to imagine this also being the case in the sixth century, potentially explaining the place name if we assume it does have a similar root meaning as Fethanlee in Oxfordshire.

The hill and the enclosure atop it would have made an ideal defensive location for the Britons, while the presence of the road cutting through it would have placed it squarely on Ceawlin's path. More than that, by sitting astride the road and challenging Ceawlin to come to them it's possible that the Britons were attacking Ceawlin's pride as a warrior. In the Early Medieval world a loss of face, such as refusing such a battle, could be deadly for a royal's ongoing ambitions.

There is one final feature of the barrows on Beacon Hill that is worth mentioning, and that is a single standing stone which seems otherwise out of place on the monument. While it is possible this was an original feature of the monument, it has also been suggested that it was moved to its present site at a later time. While it may be tempting to assign this significance as a marker of victory, such as is theorised with the Pictish Ablernmoe stones, it is impossible to say for sure. However, it is significant that stone markers like this were often used by Early Medieval armies as rally points, such as King Alfred gathering his forces at 'Egbert's Stones' prior to challenging the Danes at Ethandun. Therefore this perhaps adds some weight to the idea of Beacon Hill as a potential militarily significant site for the native Britons.

As such, Beacon Hill seems to be the most likely location for Fethanleag, although, as noted, we can never be entirely sure due to the changing nature of the landscape over time.

The final question we should consider before moving on from Fethanleag is who exactly made up Ceawlin's opponents. As is standard for the *Chronicle*, the opponent is just listed as the Britons or, often, as Wealas or 'foreigner/Latin speaker'. This makes identifying them with any level of certainty extremely difficult. Of course, there are geographical clues – as we have already seen, the battle was taking place in territory normally associated with the Durotriges tribe – though, as discussed, we have very little information about what form, if any, the tribe and its organisation took in the sixth century.

The lack of information provokes many questions. Chief among them is whether the inhabitants of the region had the military power to defeat Ceawlin and his forces alone, or whether there is reason to believe they may have had additional support from their neighbours in the west – Dumnonia.

When considering this question we first need to look at the situation from the perspective of the south-west Britons following Deorham. The post-Roman status quo they had perhaps become used to – minor Briton powers to their east and a chaotic collection of small polities in the south-east beyond that – had been replaced in a handful of years with a single Anglo-Saxon kingdom suddenly pushing westward, with a number of other similar powers taking the place of those small and easily ignored polities.

This would have been a serious cause for concern for both the Durotriges and the Dumnonians, even with their distance from events. It is not unreasonable to think that Dumnonia, likely to be the richer and more powerful of the two as we have seen previously, would look to support its longstanding neighbours to avoid having to confront the Saxons closer to home.

Certainly, at the end of the sixth century and start of the seventh there seems to be an injection of funds into the region, as this is when Glastonbury Abbey was first founded. Significantly, evidence of this early date of occupation includes imported Mediterranean pottery shards similar to those found in high-status sites throughout Dumnonia. While this doesn't mean Dumnonians built the abbey, it does indicate close trade links between the two groups which may have been closer with a single external enemy entering the region.

As such, it could be that Ceawlin found himself confronted with a larger force than that assembled by the three minor kings he'd previously defeated.

A close relationship between the Durotriges and Dumnonians may also help explain some of the missing information about the Durotriges in the post-Roman period. With Wessex pushing from the east and slowly gaining territory, as we shall see, it is possible that eventually the remnants of the Durotriges were incorporated into a single Briton state.

The final evidence for Fethanleag being a Briton victory is the simple fact that it marks the high point of Ceawlin's ambitions. While the *Chronicle* is quiet on Wessex for several years, the next entry to feature him is in 591:'This year in Britain was a great slaughter in battle at Woddesbeorg, and Ceawlin was expelled.'

It's interesting to note that in one version of the *Chronicle*, E, Ceawlin's foe is identified as the Britons; however, none of the others share this identification. Woddesbeorg or Woden's Barrow is traditionally identified as Adam's Grave in Wiltshire, back towards the heartlands of Wessex, which further makes a Briton enemy seem unlikely (again, excepting a major counter-offensive).

Barbara Yorke [1990] suggests instead that Ceawlin's opponent was his nephew Ceol, Cutha's son. Certainly in 590 there is an entry declaring that Ceol reigned for five years, and although it is not specified where he reigned it fits neatly in the gap between Ceawlin and the reign of his other nephew, Ceolwulf.

It's possible that the loss at Fethanleag and the death of Cutha weakened Ceawlin's position to the point that, when his nephews reached maturity, they were able to usurp his throne. This suggests Cutha may have been even more critical of Ceawlin's early successes than is usually credited.

There is little else we can say about the conflict between Wessex and the Britons for a few years, other than it does appear to be hotly contested. Returning to the *Chronicle*, the entry for 597 reads:

> This year Ceolwulf began to reign over the West-Saxons; and he fought and contended incessantly against either the Angles, or the Welsh, or the Picts, or the Scots. He was the son of Cutha, Cutha of Cynric, Cynric of Cerdic, Cerdic of Elesa, Elesa of Esla, Esla of Gewis, Gewis of Wig, Wig of Freawine, Freawine of Frithogar, Frithogar of Brond, Brond of Beldeg, Beldeg of Woden. This year Augustine and his companions came to the land of the Angles.

The range of Ceolwulf's enemies is interesting, although it is likely that both the Picts and Scots in this case are representative of Irish raiders attacking Wessex from its newly made border on the Severn Estuary, in the same way they had raided the older Brythonic kingdoms. Certainly the entry paints a picture of an unsettled period, and it doesn't seem that the Saxon expansion was going uncontested or, as the traditional narrative holds, the Britons were busying themselves fleeing over the sea to Brittany.

Also of note to us is the arrival of Augustine in Britain. Augustine, known after his death as the 'Apostle of the English', was sent on behalf of Pope Gregory to convert the Anglo-Saxons to Christianity. He arrived in Athelbert's court in Kent and was successful in converting the king and his nobles.

However, Augustine was unable to assert his authority (granted by the Pope) over the native Briton clergy despite meeting with some of them near the borderlands of Wessex in Somerset around the turn of the seventh century. This was the beginning of a friction that continued, in the south-west at least, right through the Early Medieval period as the British clergy refused to change their own traditions to match those of Rome.

Bede, writing about these incidents, lays the blame squarely at the Britons' feet and adds it to an overall narrative of anger against the native Church for not doing more to bring the Saxons to Christ. This does, of course, somewhat ignore the hostile relations in place between Britons and Saxons and the fact that, particularly in the Roman Church, the hierarchy of bishops had an intensely political element to it. Had the Britons accepted Augustine, it might have been seen as an acceptance of Aethelbert as king too.

Of note is that Bede records Augustine admonishing the Britons that, because they did not work to convert the Saxons, they would be ruined by the Anglo-Saxons. In Bede's narrative this prophecy comes true when Aethelfrith of Northumbria wins the Battle of Chester in the early seventh century and slaughters 1,200 Briton monks (the *Chronicle* makes this number 200 Briton priests).

While this anecdote doesn't immediately affect our tale, the obviously exaggerated detail of the monks' deaths does have a parallel in our own narrative, so it is worth including as it provides greater context for the provision of large numbers of casualties.

There seems to have been a quiet period in the West Country for a time, with Ceolwulf more concerned with conflicts with the South Saxons and other Germanic groups rather than with attempting to push further west.

Eventually Ceolwulf dies and is replaced by Cynegils, his nephew, in 611. Three years later, the *Chronicle* records the next confrontation between Wessex and the Western Britons: '614. This year Cynegils and Cuichelm fought at Beandune, and slew two thousand and sixty-five Welshmen.'

This, on the face of it, is obviously a crushing defeat of the native Britons. However, for such a defeat, remarkably little seems to change in the actual landscape of south-west Britain. Certainly there is no mention of towns conquered, and there doesn't appear to be any great expansion of English place names directly linked to this event. Further, no named kings or significant heroes seem to have died and there is no mention of it in Welsh or Irish sources.

Given that some estimates of Norman casualties at the Battle of Hastings [Marren, 2004] only just approach this figure following one of the largest battles of the age including a large and multinational force, it seems highly suspect.

Looking at it in the light of Bede's narrative of large-scale punishment of the Britons, with which the scribes of the *Chronicle* are likely to have been very familiar, it seems more likely that the figure was arrived upon precisely because it sounded impressive and better served the concept of the slothful Britons receiving a sort of heavenly retribution.

Despite this somewhat obvious piece of propaganda, Beandun is often read entirely at face value as a massive Saxon victory which effectively delivered Devon into the hands of Wessex. As discussed previously, this is somewhat typical of historians largely interested in the later history of Wessex and the Vikings who wish to accelerate the narrative. Morris [1995] and Hoskins and Finberg [1970] suggest Bindon near Axford in Devon as the site of the battle, largely relying on the naming similarity and ignoring the geographical challenges this would present in the narrative of the *Chronicle*.

If Beandun did occur it was probably a victory for the West Saxons over a significant force of Britons, perhaps even the remnants of the Durotriges' forces, that nevertheless does not seem to have conferred a speedy advance. Certainly, it would appear that the West Saxons are still on the eastern side of the Parrett judging by the subsequent battles and entries in the *Chronicle*, which we will shortly move on to. This would suggest that the most likely area for the battle is once more somewhere in central Somerset, near the Mendips and south of Bath, although this time there is not enough supplemental evidence to attempt to discern a potential location.

In the short term there appears to be a lull in activity in the west (also somewhat undermining any ideas of a sweeping, expansive victory, as this would have driven Wessex right into the heartland of Dumnonia) as inter-Saxon politics took over. Both Edwin of Northumbria and Penda of Mercia asserted their authority over Wessex at different times, and the overall politicking probably served to refocus attention on the main English regions. It's worth noting that Edwin's overlordship also included an invasion and, supposedly, the slaughter of several West Saxon kings (presumably meaning under kings of various regions like Sussex). St Birinus does arrive in 635 and is allowed to preach freely in Wessex, eventually converting the kingdom to the Roman Church.

It's not until 652 that the *Chronicle* mentions events in the West Country again, with a short entry: 'This year Kenwalh fought at Bradford on the Avon.'

There is no opponent named, and it's certainly true that Kenwalh had no shortage of Saxon enemies – he would spend many years in exile having been driven out by the Mercian king Penda – but the site of the battle at Bradford upon Avon (Bradanforda be Afene), just south of Bath and right in the border

country we have consistently identified between Wessex and the Britons suggests that he was fighting against the Britons.

Interestingly, the site of the battle being so close to Bath, coupled with the
misfortunes that had befallen Wessex over the course of the recent decades,
might suggest a counter-attack by the Britons that was threatening to seize
back lands lost following Beandun. Regardless of the reasons for the battle,
the lack of any particular accolades suggests it did not necessarily go well
for the Saxons, highlighting that the western Britons (whether Durotrigan,
Dumnonian or a confederation of both) were still able to effectively resist
Wessex's expansion.

The fairly firm citing of the battle at a place with a clear place name evolution also puts paid to any claim for earlier battles taking place in Devon. There
is simply too large a gap between the Somerset sites on the one hand, which
have the advantage of a consistent and frequent occurrence, and sites quoted
in eastern Devon which would mean crossing significant natural barriers (the
Somerset Levels, the Mendips, The Quantocks, Exmoor) for both to be true.
As such, we must again accept that Beandun is simply a lost place name somewhere in Somerset.

In 658 it was Kenwalh's turn to take the offensive, and he did:

> This year Kenwal fought with the Welsh at Pen, and pursued them to the
> Parret. This battle was fought after his return from East-Anglia, where he was
> three years in exile. Penda had driven him thither and deprived him of his
> kingdom, because he had discarded his sister.

The location of the battle appears in the Old English text as Peonnum, another
place without an obvious parallel in modern nomenclature; however, in some
translations (such as that given here) it is replaced by the Welsh toponym
'Pen', which somewhat unhelpfully simply means 'hill' (i.e. the Pennines).
Interestingly, the E version of the *Chronicle* notes the location as Penselwood, a
site in Somerset that fits the timeline extremely well and which many scholars,
though not all, now embrace.

Even if we do not accept Penselwood, though this seems the most likely
spot, there is certainly no shortage of hills in that part of Somerset. By driving the Britons to the Parrett, Kenwalh had managed to significantly shift the
border, however, achieving gains that hadn't been matched since Ceawlin's
time. At this point the Durotriges must have been absorbed into either
Dumnonia or Wessex, as the territory west of the Parrett is traditionally
viewed to be Dumnonian. However, no king is mentioned as being defeated,

nor indeed a major city taken; this seems to further support the possibility that the Durotriges had, at some point during the long interludes between fighting, become more closely integrated with Dumnonia to the point that they were essentially viewed as a single entity.

Despite the mention of the Parrett, usually proposed to be the eastern border of Dumnonia proper, there have still been proponents of a location in Devon, such as Hoskins and Finberg [1970] who propose Pinhoe in Devon, a modern-day suburb of Exeter. This is clearly extremely far west given what appears to be the pattern of events leading up to the battle. However, Hoskins and others tie themselves to a seventh-century date for the annexation of Devon in order to match timelines with the life of a Saxon saint – St Boniface.

Boniface is a fairly important figure in Early Medieval Christianity. He would eventually take on a mission to Germany and the Netherlands, the homelands of his ancestors, and attempt to convert them to Christianity. Eventually he would meet his end (so the story goes) at the hands of pagans whom he'd offended by cutting down their sacred oak. According to his official biography, the *Vitae Boniface*, compiled by his disciple Willibald sometime after his death in 754, Boniface was born in 675 somewhere in Britain to an Anglo-Saxon family. He was sent to a monastery at Exanceaster when he was a boy, at a time when Wulfhard was the abbot there.

The use of the English term for Exeter, rather than the Briton Isca or Isca Dumnorum, as well as the presence of an abbot with a Saxon name, is therefore used as proof of West Saxon control of the city at this time.

Later biographies of Boniface would take this a step further by placing his birthplace at Credeonstow or Crediton in Devon. However, this aspect is missing from the original *Vitae* and, as such, appears to be a later invention most likely tied to the Bishopric or See of Crediton, which was created at the start of the tenth century. Having a saint tied to the town would have no doubt been a great benefit for the legitimacy of the bishopric and the religious community around it.

However, there are problems with this interpretation, most notably that even if we assume the *Vitae* was completed in the year after the saint's death, this is still almost fifty years after the time Boniface would have entered monastic life. The author of the *Vitae* is likely to have written his work with a contemporary audience in mind rather than an eye for historic detail. As such, all we can say for sure is that Exeter's name was changed at some point in the latter half of the eighth century – we certainly cannot say for sure that it had changed in the seventh.

The other issue is the assumption that the monastery he entered was necessarily a Saxon one. It is worth bearing in mind at this point that the official conversion of the West Saxons only occurred in 635, and that the majority of Church apparatus was based around the diocesan seat at Dorchester. While the bishop's seat will eventually move to Winchester, both of these locations are very far to the east of Exeter.

The western seat of Sherborne, still a good way from Exeter, won't actually be founded until 705, suggesting the Wessex Church was expanding slowly from the east and certainly would not be in the position to support a monastery in what would, even with Hoskins's very generous timeline, be the very hinterland of their royal patron's power.

Instead, it seems more likely that the monastery Boniface entered, if it was indeed in Exeter, was probably a long-standing Briton institution. Indeed, we know from another saint, St Aldhelm of Malmesbury, that there were at least some institutions of that nature in Dumnonia and Cornwall in this time period. He notes a particular incident in his poetic letter, the *Carmen Rhythmicum*, when he was travelling 'Through Dire Dumnonia and bare Cornubia' and had stopped at a religious house in the region during a storm.

While celebrating matins, indicating this was likely to be a monastery, the storm blew the roof off the church and caused significant damage to the building. There are several things about this incident which are of interest, both to our general narrative and to the specific timelines at question in the late seventh century.

Firstly, as mentioned, it reinforces the presence of religious houses in the Brittonic west at the time that Boniface would likely be receiving his initial religious training. Secondly, it shows that – while the British and English Churches had significant differences in practice for which we must revisit Aldhelm shortly – there was still communication and even travel between the two institutions during this time. This means that finding a Saxon abbot , such as Wulfhard, in a theoretically Briton monastery is not only entirely possible but also extremely likely.

Particularly if we bear in mind the already noted slow expansion of the Wessex Church, it may well be that early Christian adopters in the westernmost regions of the new West Saxon kingdom were drawn to Briton institutions in the practice of their faith. This would counter the narrative Bede supposes of a standoffish Briton Church, but would perhaps make more sense on a more local level where issues of control and baptismal precedence were not as pressing. This also adds to the image of a Dumnonian state that is more outward looking and engaged in trade, which we have seen throughout this book.

The final item to consider is the distinction Aldhelm draws between Dumnonia and Cornwall. This may indicate, as the archaeology supports, that the infrastructure of the kingdom was different across the two regions, or may suggest a longstanding tribal differentiation underneath the overall Dumnonian banner.

This is also the first separate mention of Cornwall within the Early Medieval period, as well as being amongst the clearest specifically dealing with the inhabitants of the south-west peninsula. Older references, particularly pre-Roman ones, can sometimes be difficult to place, the root word 'Corn' simply meaning horn or spit of land. Thus there are many candidate sites for Cornovii references. Having this clear identifier of a potential separate Cornish identity can help flesh out the complex identities of Early Medieval people that we have only touched on earlier; it further supports the idea of layered identities where a national, regional and sub-regional identity may all mix in a given individual.

With the higher occurrence of finds and significant high-status infrastructure in Cornwall, it also raises interesting questions around how and where the two sub-regions identified by Aldhelm became united as a single Dumnonian kingdom. It is of course possible that Aldhelm is actually identifying two separate political units rather than merely regions. However, given the way he addresses his later letter to King Geraint, as Lord of the Western Kingdom, it seems unlikely that the intention is to identify two separate realms but instead may refer to a more geographic or traditional separation.

There is further support for a Dumnonia of small tribal units from an earlier source, the *Life of St Samson*, which is a Breton hagiography for the eponymous saint. During his travels from Demetae in Wales to Brittany, he passes through Cornwall and instructs the followers of a local war leader in proper Christian practices. The title of the war leader is the Latin *Comes*, which bears with it an assumption of deputised power rather than independence. This may suggest a Dumnonia made up of many separate pieces united under a 'high king' or overlord in a manner similar to Irish examples.

With that in mind, however, the inclusion of both regions as areas to journey through indicates that a significant amount of territory is still outside of West Saxon control, making a seizure of Devon extremely unlikely.

There is one final battle to close out this early stage of conflict between Dumnonia and Wessex, and it is another ambiguous entry in the *Chronicle* about which much has been made. The entry is for 682: 'In this year Centwine drove the Britons to the sea.'

As we have seen throughout, the level of ambiguity in the *Chronicle* can lead to dozens of interpretations for this entry. For those seeking to accelerate the timeline for the conquest of Devon this has been taken to mean a full-scale sweeping away of the old Briton order. In *The Westward Expansion of Wessex*, Hoskins and Finberg [1970] put it as follows:

> The Battle of 682 was fought in a place which will never be identified, but the phrase about driving the Britons as far as the sea becomes clear and unequivocal if we locate this unnamed battle somewhere west of the Taw and north of Dartmoor. As a result of a crushing defeat, the British were pushed westwards to the very coast of the Atlantic, into what is now north-east Cornwall. With the battle of 682 the West Saxons virtually completed their conquest of the eastern half of Dumnonia, the part that later became the county of Devon.

Not only does this ignore the evidence so far discussed which places Wessex at the Parrett, but it is also self-defeating if taken at face value. If we accept his premise of a location north of Dartmoor and west of the Taw, and select Hatherleigh in Devon and go straight west towards Bude on the north Cornish coastline, then it is a distance of 20 miles as the crow flies.

Twenty miles of, particularly at the time, extremely rough terrain is an extraordinary distance to drive a defeated army in the literal way Hoskins interprets. This would be true for almost any force, but particularly given the more limited use of cavalry employed by Anglo-Saxon armies when compared to their Briton opponents, at least so far as we can tell in their respective heroic literature.

This rather grandstanding placement and distance also ignores the reality of south-western Britain as a peninsula where you are never particularly far from the sea.

In an effort to combat this narrative, then, we have to look again at potential other placements for the conflict in 682. In the first instance we need to consider whether Centwine is likely to have been fighting the Dumnonians at all. In this we are not aided particularly by the *Chronicle's* use of Welsh, or Wealas to use the Old English. This is a general term for a foreigner or, potentially, Latin-speaker. With earlier entries this ambiguity makes events harder to place due to the more chaotic nature of politics in the centuries following Roman withdrawal. However, by this point the status quo of Anglo-Saxon kingdoms had become more formalised, and while Wessex pushed westward they were equally pressured from their northern and eastern borders, particularly by the powerful kingdoms of Mercia and Northumbria.

There is, of course, the possibility that the foreigners in question were Irish raiders, as have been mentioned in the past both in Dumnonia and early entries of the *Chronicle*. However, in general the Wealas term seems to be used only in relation to native Britons, with the Irish sometimes interchangeably referred to as Irish, Picts or Scots, but not Wealas. This potentially supports a hypothesis that the term is more complex than simply 'foreigner'.

So when this is all borne in mind, Dumnonia does seem the natural opponent for the battle in 682. We can then use the Parrett as a potential starting point, given its identification earlier in the *Chronicle* and the natural border it provides. The terrain surrounding the Parrett is extremely rough and difficult to move through, even in the modern day. Flooding in 2015 swamped the major routes through the region and effectively cut off Devon and Cornwall from the rest of the UK. As we have seen, modern roads are often reflective of longer-standing historical networks, so this would likely have been a fairly common occurrence in earlier ages.

The Somerset Levels in particular would have provided a significant natural barrier in the region, while the Quantocks similarly prevent easy movement through the region. This means there are only two routes that it is likely someone would attempt to move significant forces through, whether the aggressor in this case was Dumnonian or Saxon.

To eliminate the least likely first, it is possible that forces could be moved along the southern coastline and then upwards from there once the terrain on either side becomes more favourable. This has the advantage of being potentially more stable and also allowing for support from ships, if they were available. However, it would mean, in both cases, leaving a path potentially open towards an important site, Glastonbury Abbey and Isca Dumnorum both being within a few days' march of the Parrett. For Wessex it would also mean moving forces southwards at a time when pressure from Mercia and potentially from Kent is building.

It therefore seems more likely that the conflict would have occurred somewhere close to the other path, the gap between the Quantocks and Blackdown hills where Taunton now sits. This is also where most modern routes, including the M5 motorway, now cross from Somerset into Devon. When we look at sites in this region – Bridgewater, for example – the claims about driving the Britons into the sea also make a good deal more sense. On the one hand the Levels, being at least partially salt water estuarine on their northern end, may have been considered close enough to sea by the distant writers of the *Chronicle*, making any battle in the region that ended in a rout likely to result in the losers being 'driven to the sea'.

On the other hand, if we take the phrase entirely at face value, then we can get a distance of around 4–5 miles directly north before we reach the Irish

Sea. This is obviously a far more manageable distance to pursue a foe if we are being entirely literal. Certainly it is more realistic than covering 20 miles of rough ground.

Whatever the exact details were, the battle in 682 marks an ending to this initial chapter of confrontation between Wessex and Dumnonia. While the Saxon kingdom has not always had things its own way, it has inexorably drawn closer to Dumnonia year on year, swallowing territory that was once in the hands of seemingly friendly neighbours and potentially client states.

Wessex had, in the minds of the Dumnonian elite at least, transformed from a distant and ill-defined collection of newcomers to the largest single threat to their continued ability to rule and trade as they had been doing since the time of the Romans. With the conflict now at their doorstep, they would have been forced to act in order to preserve their own interests.

At the same time, as Aldhelm's ill-fated journey and the Saxon abbot of Isca Dumnorum show us, the newfound closeness of the two states was not only a source of conflict. It was also bringing together both sides and leading to an increasing exchange of people and ideas. The very first sparks of cooperation may well have emerged from this fractious period.

To understand how the Dumnonian elite reacted to this new situation, we need to look at perhaps the best documented Dumnonian king we have, Geraint of Dumnonia, and how his actions affected the wider relationship between the two states.

6

KING GERAINT, LLONGBORTH AND THE BATTLE THAT SAVED CORNWALL

The existence of a King Geraint is attested in four separate sources. The first is a letter addressed to him from Aldhelm, whom we have introduced previously. Aldhelm appears to have been instructed by a gathering of priests from all over Britain to attempt to bring the Dumnonian Church into compliance with what might be called the Roman rites, specifically the calculation of Easter Day and the tonsure worn by priests and monks.

It is notable that the opening tone of Aldhelm's letter is largely conciliatory and deferent. This does not appear to be the instructions of a conqueror over a cowed people but instead an appeal to a figure that Aldhelm clearly believes possesses the power to make the changes he argues for.

He addresses Geraint as the 'glorious lord of the Western Kingdom' and extends fond greetings to him and to all the priests of Dumnonia. It should be made clear at this point that Aldhelm is a famously erudite user of Latin and there is some significance to the fact that all of his stylistic flair is on display here. Not only is it a display of his own education and, tacitly at least, deployed in support of his arguments, but it also shows he clearly believed that Geraint himself or those around him would be able to read and understand the message and complex themes woven into it well enough that there was no need for simpler language.

Additionally this does show that, for all the long-running conflict and the long years since Roman withdrawal, there remains a single powerful elite within Dumnonia around whom the traditional infrastructure of power, including the local Church hierarchy, is gathered.

According to Aldhelm, the variance has occurred because the local priests are following in the traditions of their founders and ancestors rather than accepting the Roman calculation. This could be seen as another expression of identity in the face of a growing and alien status quo in Britain. Aldhelm sees this clinging to tradition as wrong-headed and repeatedly puts forward ideas of Christian unity and brotherhood as being more important than the local traditions, as well as citing the legitimacy of Peter in order to override them. These sections, given the richness of the language used, are open to considerable interpretation. For while Aldhelm seems keen not to offend, often speaking of 'rumours' he'd heard rather than specifically blaming Geraint or any particular priest for the failings, there is an underlying thread of warning.

Aldhelm's repeated references to singular Christian unity, as well as a number of other minor inserts (such as referring to Dumnonia as a 'Province' rather than a kingdom), seem to carry with them an element of unspoken threat: correct this error or else be corrected.

In the wake of the defeat in 682, this is likely to have been a message understood even if not directly expressed, and certainly both the letter and Aldhelm's journey speak to a period in Dumnonia–Wessex relations when there was at least some room for discussion and diplomacy.

Indeed, as Probert [2002] notes in his study of south-west place names, there appears to be a growing influx of English-speaking settlers in eastern Devon around this time. The lack of Brittonic elements in their settlement names seems to suggest they were founding new farms or villages rather than taking over existing ones. These newcomers should perhaps be seen as the latest in a long line of settlers that Dumnonia and its far-spanning trade network welcomed in, the town names perhaps viewed in the same light as the Ogham stones that marked Irish settlement several centuries earlier.

This is supported by another of the sources to mention Geraint (or 'Gerent' in this source), an undated charter granting land at Maker (across the Tamar from Plymouth) to the abbey at Sherborne [Probert, 2010]. While the surviving charter is much later, it is widely believed to be legitimate and as such may represent a diplomatic overture by Geraint or the Dumnonian Church towards Aldhelm and, by extension, the West Saxon state.

This would seem to indicate that Aldhelm's efforts were at least partially successful. While there would remain differences in the practice of the Church for at least a short time longer, Bede notes towards the end of his *Ecclesiastical History* that Aldhelm's letter 'Caused many Britons to accept the proper calculation of Easter' (Easter being the more urgent matter to both Aldhelm's and Bede's minds). However, it is equally possible that the grant was made as a token of goodwill to forestall the implied threat that undercuts much of the flowery language.

Either way, it is perhaps notable that conflict between the two sides did not resume until after Aldhelm's death in 709. It suggests that Aldhelm may well have been committed to bringing the two sides, both Church and lay, together peacefully in brotherhood as he often notes. As a senior bishop in Wessex, his influence may have been significant enough to forestall further acts of aggression westward.

Of course, Aldhelm's passing was not the only change to occur in Wessex during the changeover from the seventh to eighth centuries. A long period of political instability, replete with burnings, civil wars and rulers in exile, came to an end in 688 with the ascension of King Ine (or Ina) to the throne of Wessex.

Ine was an energetic and powerful king, though he was unable to match some of the military successes of his predecessors in subjugating other Saxon realms. He did negotiate a significant tribute from Kent in response to the death of Mul, one of his predecessors in the royal family, and consolidated Wessex's position on the southern bank of the Thames. Bede notes he was also able to control Sussex for a time, though evidently this was not a permanent state of affairs.

In 694, Ine also issued the first set of laws of any Saxon ruler outside of Kent. It is notable that Ine's laws set out separate rules for his English (the word 'Englisc' is used here, indicating the slow start of a shared cultural identity) and Wealas subjects. Notably, the rules are entirely in favour of the former group, often at the expense of the latter. Despite being a fervent Christian, Ine doesn't appear to have the same vision of a single brotherhood that Aldhelm (at least purported) to espouse.

This clearly shows that, while Wessex had absorbed significant Briton regions and people in the last 100 years or so of expansion, it still thought of them as an 'other' even within the kingdom. This contrasts with more modern thinking about the Anglo-Saxon period, which relies on a peaceful take up of Anglo-Saxon culture by the natives.

Interestingly, it also hints that the native Britons were retaining their own culture and identities in the face of the political changes going on around them, something which has been difficult if not impossible to prove through the archaeological record.

In 710, Ine was on the offensive, and we find the third source to mention Geraint in the *Anglo-Saxon Chronicle*: 'Ina and Nun his kinsman fought against

Gerent king of the Welsh; and the same year Higbald was slain.' ('Nun' is also translated as Nothelm, King of Sussex and subject of Ine.)

While the term 'Welsh' or 'Wealas' once again leaves significant ambiguity, we can again be relatively certain, given the political state and borders of the Saxon kingdoms, that Dumnonia is the only sensible opponent in this battle. It is also interesting to note here that Gerent is named as 'King of the Welsh', making clear that he was a singular leader west of the Parrett.

While with previous battles we had little else to go on besides the *Chronicle*, there is another source in this case that can help shed light not just on the battle itself but on the location of it.

The eleventh-century poem *Geraint ab Erbin* (*Geraint, son of Erbin*) records a heroic Geraint fighting at a place called Llongborth:

In Llongborth I saw the rage of slaughter,
And biers beyond all number,
And red-stained men from the assault of Geraint.

In Llongborth I saw the edges of blades in contact,
Men in terror and blood on the pate,
Before Geraint, the great son of his father.

The poem is found in the *Black Book of Carmarthen*, one of the major sources for Early Medieval Welsh literature. While it does not date the battle, it does specify Geraint's origin as 'the region of Dyvnaint' which is the Old Welsh word for Devon (Cornish: Dewnans). This, together with the other historical sources identifying both a real Geraint and his conflict with Wessex, would seem to be a clear indication that the poem is referring to Geraint of Dumnonia.

This seems even more clear-cut when we consider that Langport in Somerset sits right in the Taunton gap we previously identified as the most likely place for conflicts between the two sides. While there is limited evidence of occupation at Langport until the later ninth century, that does not mean the name was not already in use, albeit in an older form.

Certainly this has all been enough to convince some academics like Skene [1988] of the link between Geraint and Geraint ab Erbin. However, there remains significant discussion and controversy around this link.

To understand why, we need to discuss a figure who has been notably, and perhaps surprisingly, absent from consideration until now: King Arthur.

Arthurian mythology casts a long shadow in the West Country, with folk stories having built up over time to cement Cornwall as 'Arthur's Homeland' in the minds of many visitors and students of the tales. In this, *Geraint ab Erbin* is partially to blame. The poem includes a single line referencing Arthur, using his (by the eleventh century, already growing) mythos as a kenning or allegory for bravery and noble leadership:

> In Llongborth I saw Arthur,
> And brave men who hewed down with steel,
> Emperor, and conductor of the toil.

A single line may not seem like much, but outside the works of Nennius which we've already mentioned, this is amongst the earliest mentions of Arthur in a historical source. As such, there is much more focus on it than its contents perhaps deserve.

Over time Geraint was woven into the wider Arthurian mythos, particularly in Geraint and Enid, one of the three Welsh romances of the fourteenth century. It is particularly notable that, despite claims from some scholars that Geraint and Enid comes directly from some lost older source, it is largely identifiable as an adaptation of the French work *Erec and Enid* by Chrétien de Troyes.

Geraint's newfound fame also saw him edited into several genealogies during the High Medieval period as a figure of the fifth or sixth centuries. This has led to modern interpretations of *Gerain ab Erbin* as relating to a much earlier battle in order to tie the historical Geraint into the mythology built around his fictional shadow.

This offers a snapshot of the wider problem that the Arthurian mythos presents when attempting to study the Early Medieval period in the West Country. Because the shadow of Arthur is so all-encompassing, it can, and has for many years, bury a fascinating historical truth beneath layers of obscuring myth and storytelling which have, by dint of many years' retelling, taken on the sheen of validity.

Having spent time looking at the relation between the Western Kingdom and the expanding spheres of Anglo-Saxon influence, it should be extremely clear that, if we accept that there was at some point a historical Arthur leading Briton resistance to the incoming Saxons in the fifth century, then he would have been considerably further east or north than Dumnonia, let alone Cornwall.

Indeed, the use of his name as a kenning in a poem commemorating a battle at the edge of Devon in the eighth century if we assume the 11th century written version worked from an earlier oral source, strongly suggests he was already enshrined in the shared cultural mythos of the Britons long before Devon and Cornwall saw a hint of Anglo-Saxon rule.

So we can dismiss any claims of a significantly earlier battle, as most of these rely heavily on mythological sources for their basis. There has been some suggestion that the battle described may relate to a separate battle in northern England, near the Briton kingdom of Strathclyde where a tribal group known as the Damnonii dwelt. This placement, however, relies on several assumptions that don't string together well.

To begin with, although the obvious similarity between Damnonii and Dumnonii seems straightforward, the poem never actually uses Dumnonia in its identification of Geraint or of the battle site, only the Old Welsh word for Devon. Additionally, although there had previously been kings of Strathclyde named Geraint and the *Welsh Annals* note in 722 that Beli son of Elfin dies, which could, potentially, be a mutation of Erbin, there is nothing to suggest that this is the case or that he has a brother called Geraint.

All of this returns us not only to the eighth century and the historical Geraint we have identified, but also to Langport in Somerset as the most likely location for the battle commemorated in the *Chronicle* and in *Geraint ab Erbin*. It is the only site that fits both the site named within the poem and the geographic region we have identified the continuing conflict to be centred around.

Unfortunately for Geraint, this also means (per the poem) that Langport is the place he met his end:

> In Llongborth Geraint was slain,
> A brave man from the region of Dyvnaint,
> And before they were overpowered, they committed slaughter.

As a final consideration, it is shortly after the battle that Taunton is constructed, straddling this gap in the natural barriers of West Somerset. The *Chronicle* notes for 722: 'This year queen Ethelburga razed Taunton, which Ina had previously built; and Ealdbert the exile departed into Surrey and Sussex, and Ina fought against the South-Saxons.'

This is the earliest mention of Taunton, indicating its construction (by Ine) was relatively recent. Taunton is recognised later as a 'burh' or fortified settlement so it seems likely this was its original purpose too. The fact that the rebellious Ealdbert starts at Taunton and then flees east is interesting – perhaps he had hoped to drum up support from the Britons but the destruction of Taunton robbed him of the chance. This would actually make some sense of the action, as it would deny the fortress to any Briton forces that may have come to his aid and thus made them easier to push back.

As for why a burh would be built here, that too should be obvious, and reinforces that victory at Llongborth is the moment when the West Saxons were able to push through Somerset and into eastern Devon. By securing the gap at Taunton behind him, Ine was in effect entirely in control of the main routes in and out of the south-west peninsula, and also had a fortified site to retreat to should anything go wrong.

The Saxon victory at Llongborth is a hugely significant turning point in the history of the south-west generally and Cornwall in particular. With the intimidating natural barriers of western Somerset now gone, it would not have taken long for the victorious West Saxons to stream into eastern Devon. The fact that Llongborth was the latest in a short series of military defeats would have also severely taxed the ability of local forces to resist the expansion.

In short, Dumnonia more or less dies with Geraint at Llongborth, at least as a unified entity. With the Saxons now moving freely into Devon there was also a not insignificant chance that Cornwall would also be overwhelmed.

However, in 722, the same year Taunton is being destroyed, the *Annales Cambriae* or *Welsh Annals* record the following event:

> *Et bellum Hehil apud Cornuenses, Gueith Gartmailauc, Cat Pencon, apud dex-terales Brittones, et Brittones victores fuerunt in istis tribus bellis.*
>
> And the battle of Hehil among the Cornish, the battle of Garth Maelog, the battle of Pencon among the south Britons, and the Britons were the victors in those three battles.

Just a single line, but a hugely significant moment for Cornish history. Not only is this one of the first sources to identify Cornwall and the Cornish not just as a region or sub-division of Dumnonia, but it also reverses the momentum Wessex had built up in its westward march.

It is perhaps significant to note here that the way Geraint is described in *Geraint ab Erbin* as 'from the region of Dynvaint' potentially links him specifically to a royal family ruling from Isca Dumnorum, and with his death the power base in the region decisively shifted to the west, which, as we have seen, had more significant infrastructure in place.

Given that Cornwall is already identifiable as a separate regional identity, as evidenced in Aldhelm's writings and here in the *Annals*, it is perhaps notable that the battle is 'among the Cornish' rather than 'within Cornwall' or similar. This may support the idea that the battle was geographically located not in modern-day Cornwall but rather in territory that was now controlled by the Cornish branch of the formerly unified Dumnonia.

Certainly, the Britons would have been extremely keen to keep hold of much of Devon, in particular Dartmoor and the tin deposits there. These were, in fact, undergoing something of a rapid expansion, as evidenced by increased isotope production noted in recent studies [Meharg et al., 2012]. Additionally, much of the good grazing and pasture land for horses (again, including Dartmoor) was also in Devon, and given the importance of the horse to the way the warrior elite not only conducted war but also to how they saw themselves as warriors, this would have been a serious loss.

While some commentators have pointed to the lack of a named opponent, and the absence of these battles from the *Chronicle*, as reasons to either doubt their existence or else suggest they were potentially civil in nature ('among the Cornish'), it would seem a much more sensible suggestion that the opponent is not named because, for the Welsh writers, there was only a single enemy it could be – the expanding Anglo-Saxon states.

As for why the three battles are missing from the *Anglo-Saxon Chronicle*, we have already seen that the writers of the *Chronicle* are often coy with details of battles where the outcomes may not be beneficial to their own narratives (such as Feathenleag), so omitting a series of military defeats would seem entirely in keeping with this approach.

Siting this battle is extremely difficult given the lack of information. It is equally hard to say what truly occurred, although many have tried. In general, these efforts have been hampered by a literal interpretation of the single source. The phrase 'among the Cornish' has too often been used to move the site of the battle deep into modern-day Cornwall, particularly around Hayle in West Cornwall and at various sites around the River Camel and its estuary [Hoskins and Finberg, 1970].

However, all of these sites assume that the defeat at Llongborth delivered all of Devon to West Saxon hands at the same time. This does not seem likely given the pattern of relatively slow expansion that came before it, as well as the importance of the territory to the Cornish. Certainly we should not sugar coat the loss at Llongborth – as noted, the defeat effectively spelled the end of Dumnonia as a unified kingdom and almost certainly was swiftly followed by the seizure of Exeter, thus leading to the city's English designation in the *Vitae Boniface* as discussed earlier.

However, we equally shouldn't accept a narrative of acquiescence, of the Cornish now fading into the background after all the long years of resistance that have come before. Given all they had to lose, it seems much more likely they would have dug in and resisted as much as they could.

Other commentators like Malcolm Todd [1987] suggest instead that we should seek the battlefield further east, suggesting either Hele, near Jacobstow in north-east Cornwall, or Hele in the Culm Valley, Devon. While neither of these sites seems entirely convincing on their own, it is interesting to note that Hele is a fairly common place name in the south-west, even in the later period.

The *Exon Book* – the collection of documents which fed information about south-west Britain to the Domesday Book of William the Conqueror – lists four Heles at the time of its compilation in the 1080s. This includes both the Cornish and Culm Valley example, although the latter is included in the hundred of Taunton rather than Devon proper. Of particular interest for us is an entry for the hundred of Merton, in central Devon: 'The count of Mortain holds 1 estate which is called Hele, which 2 thegns held jointly on the day that King Eadweard was alive and dead, and they could go to any lord they wished with that land.'

Merton is today a small village to the north of Okehampton and close to the River Torridge. Its position in the centre of Devon, as well as a close proximity to the important Anglo-Saxon town of Crediton, gives it potentially excellent credentials as the site for the historic Hehil. This would both match a slow and contested invasion of Devon and also make sense in the context of the time.

While today we would probably assume the south coast of Devon is the obvious choice, as this is where our roads travel – from Exeter to Plymouth and then onwards – most of the large coastal towns were built in the early modern period, and Devon's agricultural heartland would have had much more value to a largely agrarian society such as existed in the eighth century. Even Bantham, the former trading port, seems to be abandoned around this time, suggesting that the fighting had grown close enough to make trade less profitable than it would be at the smaller coastal sites around the Cornish coast such as Gwithian.

A victory here would have kept the fighting in Devon, preserving the Cornish heartland from an invasion as well as directly impeding the West Saxons. Certainly it seems that conflict remained constant in the following years, as the Chronicle records:

753. This year Cuthred, king of the West-Saxons, fought against the Welsh
755. ….And Cynewulf fought very many hard battles against the Welsh.

If we place the majority of this fighting around western and central Devon, then the importance of Hehil is even more clear: what had been a continuous expansion has now been mired down and once again slowed.

Interestingly, this narrative of a slower Saxon expansion recently received a boost from researchers looking at the genetic makeup of the modern UK as part of the People of the British Isles project run by the University of Oxford. Early analysis of the samples in the data set has shown significant clustering of what might be called 'English' genetics roughly where they would be expected – that is, in south and eastern England though to Somerset.

However, samples taken from people in Cornwall and Devon/West Somerset both present with genetic signatures that are separate to the baseline 'English' sample. More than that, they are different from one another, suggesting that there was either a pre-existing difference between the groups, or that one group (Devon/West Somerset) was subjected to an injection of people with different genetic markers at some point in the past [Leslie et al., 2015]. While we must be careful with genetic studies of this type – they certainly are not the foolproof science of origins often touted by companies offering to share with people their 'genetic heritage' – they can be useful in identifying very broad-stroke population trends, such as the marker differences noted here.

Also of note is a charter issued by Cynewulf to Wells Monastery in 776 [Sawyer, S262] which mentions 'harassment of our enemies of the Cornish nation', although whether Cynewulf was fighting the Cornish at the time he issued the charter or else giving thanks for a victory is not immediately clear. This does, however, show that the conflict was continuing even late in the eighth century.

The close of the eighth century can be seen as the end of this first era of relationships between Wessex and the Western Kingdom – what was Dumnonia and now was the Kingdom of Cerniu, the old Cornish term that will one day evolve into the better-known Kernow.

We have seen that, while many historians would seek to push the story to the modern borders of the Tamar as fast as possible, it is a story of conflict and resistance that is worthy of retelling, not just for the spirited resistance the Britons were able to put up, but also for the achievements of the West Saxons. For all that they were the invaders, they were also the weaker party when they began to move west. Thanks to some key victories, and perhaps some luck, they were able to change this position so that by the start of the ninth century they had the stronger hand – though the Cornish were by no means beaten just yet.

As for the nature of the Cornish kingdom itself, we have only the vaguest of ideas. We do know that the royal court, previously based at large fortresses like Tintagel, probably took on at least some measure of mobility. The place-name element 'Lys', such as is found today in Liskeard, donates a 'court' or law-site that the king would attend with his nobles to hear pleas and dispense judgement. This model of mobile kingship has strong parallels in Early Medieval Wales, where ideas of kingship and rule were based much more individually on rulers and the Teylu they commanded than on specific geographic areas.

While Cornwall overall is a more settled, and less volatile, kingdom by this point at the dawn of the ninth century, it is also undoubtedly still a Brythonic one, and as such would be expected to share these elements with its cousins in Brittany and Wales. Still, it is perhaps worth noting that the landscape which surrounds Liskeard is one of multiple ancient monuments from the Neolithic and Bronze Age. It is also a crossroads in Cornwall, a place where travel from the east tends to naturally flow. As such, it marks a natural spot to find the royal household. This suggests the possibility that, while the king may well have moved from site to site, this was a more settled pattern or routine than in other kingdoms.

7

THE WARS ENDING: ECGBERHT AND THE FINAL CLASHES

We have seen, in the long narrative of Wessex's western push, that the actions of individual rulers can sometimes have an enormous impact on the fate of the south-west as a whole. Many of these figures, like Ceawlin and Ine, are little known today outside of those with a particular interest in the Early Medieval period, despite all their accomplishments added to the eventual emergence of a single, unified England under the Kings of Wessex.

At this point we need to introduce perhaps the most important of these forgotten kings, certainly the one who has the largest single hand in setting Wessex on the path that will eventually see it dominate all of England.

Unfortunately, at least from the viewpoint of the Western Kingdom, he is also the one who will effectively end the military resistance in Cornwall, although this is not the same as completing its conquest.

With all that being said, things didn't actually start very promisingly for the young Ecgberht. He was, it is believed, the eldest son of the King of Kent, and related to the royal line of Wessex from several generations back via King Ine's brother. The Britain Ecgberht was born into, that of the late eighth century, was dominated by a single Anglo-Saxon kingdom and its king: Offa of Mercia.

Offa was a warrior king in every sense of the word and he had used his military might and talent to extract tribute or subjugate almost all of his neighbours at one time or another. Cynewulf of Wessex seems to have resisted Offa's attempts to raise himself as overlord but he was murdered in 786 by another noble who then also died. A relatively unknown descendant of Cerdic, named Beohtric, then ascended to the throne of Wessex.

While it isn't clear whether Offa had a direct hand in Cynewulf's death, he certainly seems to have been the real power behind Beohtric's rule, going so far as to marry Beohtric to his daughter, Eadburh. Soon, lands that had traditionally been within Wessex were being administered from the Mercian court and issued out in charters by Offa himself, while Mercian currency appears to become the nominal currency of Wessex as well.

It seems clear that this situation was working well for Offa and neither he, nor his puppet king, would want a challenger with stronger (or at least more recent) links to the royal line of Wessex abroad in the country. As such, they conspired to send the young Ecgberht into exile in Frankia, where he attended the court of Charlemagne.

William of Malmesbury, writing long after events but sometimes considered to have had access to earlier sources that we lack, attests it was in Charlemagne's court that Ecgberht learned how to rule:

> Egbert, passing the sea, went into France; a circumstance which I attribute to the counsels of God, that a man destined to rule so great a kingdom might learn the art of government from the Franks; for this people has no competitor among all the Western nations in military skill or polished manners. This ill-treatment Egbert used as an incentive to 'rub off the rust of indolence,' to quicken the energy of his mind, and to adopt foreign customs, far differing from his native barbarism.

It should be noted that William is a highly unreliable narrator, whatever sources he may have had access to, though in this case he may have had more of a point than in his other writings. Charlemagne was engaged in building a highly 'modern' and effective state in what would one day become France and Germany while also undertaking great endeavours to spread Christianity to the still-pagan populations of north-west Europe – whether they wanted it or not.

Even if Charlemagne did not have a direct hand in Ecgberht's education, being within the court of the most powerful man in Europe would have done wonders for his future chances as he was able to build support for his claim with powerful and influential figures.

Certainly, when Beohtric died at the turn of the ninth century Ecgberht seemed to waste no time in returning from exile to ascend the throne. It's unclear whether Charlemagne or figures in his court directly supported his return, but it seems reasonable to assume that at least the image of their friendship is likely to have discouraged any other claimants within Wessex, even if it did nothing to deter aggression from Mercia. As the *Chronicle* records:

This year was the moon eclipsed, at eight in the evening, on the seventeenth day before the calends of February; and soon after died King Bertric and Alderman Worr. Egbert succeeded to the West-Saxon kingdom; and the same day Ethelmund, alderman of the Wiccians, rode over the Thames at Kempsford; where he was met by Alderman Woxtan, with the men of Wiltshire, and a terrible conflict ensued, in which both the commanders were slain, but the men of Wiltshire obtained the victory.

The 'Wiccians' or men of Hwicce were originally an independent kingdom from the borderlands between Wessex and Mercia, although by this time they had been fully absorbed as part of the Mercian state. It seems unlikely that their aggression was an independent action – instead, it was presumably meant as an embarrassment of the new king. After all, the central role of the king is as the protector of his people. If Ecgberht had failed to respond to the incursion so soon after his crowning, he would have been shamed.

As it is, this is the last conflict noted between Wessex and Mercia for close to twenty years, suggesting that, while Wessex's ealdorman also died, the overall battle had gone poorly for the invaders. By this time Offa himself was dead, and his heir Coenwulf was on Mercia's throne. He had previously maintained his father's control over Wessex via Beohtric, but he was not able to subdue Ecgberht so easily.

Much of the time between conflicts with Mercia was spent on events in the west, to which we will return shortly, but in order to give further context both to Ecgberht and some of what will follow we need to discuss his most stunning victory. In 825, Ecgberht met the forces of Mercia at Ellandun:

Egbert king of the West-Saxons and Bernulf king of the Mercians fought at Ellandun, and Egbert got the victory, and there was great slaughter made. He then sent from the army his son Ethelwulf, and Ealstan his bishop, and Wulfherd his ealdorman, into Kent with a large force, and they drove Baldred the king northwards over the Thames. And the men of Kent, and the men of Surrey, and the South-Saxons, and the East-Saxons, submitted to him; for formerly they had been unjustly forced from his kin. And the same year the king of the East-Angles and the people sought the alliance and protection of king Egbert for dread of the Mercians; and the same year the East-Angles slew Bernulf king of Mercia.

This is followed in 827 by an entry stating that Ecgberht not only conquers Mercia but also receives the submission of the Northumbrian kings, though this later statement is hotly debated, and has instead been suggested to be a more general discussion to avoid conflict.

The implications of Ellandun are enormous. Not only does the battle leave Ecgberht in a position to claim dominion over almost all of England for a short time (he is unable to retain all the territorial gains he achieves), but it also permanently transfers the ownership of all of southern England; the previously independent kingdoms of Kent, Sussex and Essex all become part of Wessex and remain there. This provides Wessex with a strong, wealthy base with which it will meet the looming crisis of the Great Heathen Army.

It is extremely likely without Ecgberht and his victories that the collection of smaller kingdoms would have been unable to rise to the challenge in the same way as the singular Wessex state, regardless of Alfred's undeniable skill as a leader.

Ellandun also highlights that Ecgberht was a successful military leader. Even without Offa and Coenwulf at the head, the Mercian forces would have been the dominant military force in Britain at the time. To come out of exile and defeat them in only twenty years is an incredible success story and one that we will see reflected in other conflicts in the West Country.

Of course, if you are going to lose, it is at least some comfort to be beaten by someone so skilled.

We have seen that conflict in Devon was a significant recurring feature of the late eighth century, but Cynewulf's death seems to put a temporary pause on the conflict. Given the close links between Beohtric and Offa, it is possible that the focus during these years, from the Saxon point of view, was more on conflicts within 'England' as well as Offa's frequent invasions and suppressions of the various Welsh princes on Mercia's western borders.

Ecgberht, on the other hand, was presumably keen to expand his own powerbase before attempting to challenge Mercia militarily, a long-term goal which he must have borne in mind throughout his rule.

In 813 the *Chronicle* records that he is on the offensive in one of the most infamous, for Cornwall certainly, passages in the entire recording: 'King Egbert spread devastation in Cornwall from east to west.'

This is frequently interpreted as a campaign that took the entirety of Cornwall into his dominion, or at least it suffered from his campaign [Kirby, 1992]; however, this is difficult to square with the longer-running conflicts we've seen over the preceding century. Additionally, if Wessex is able to so easily dominate the entirety of Cornwall, then we would expect the conflict to end here and potentially Cornwall's unique identity to more or less vanish, in the way that Devon's Brythonic origins are now only vaguely remembered. Obviously neither of these things occur.

Of course, even the *Chronicle* doesn't actually state he conquered the region either, only that he went raiding or harrying: 'spreading devastation'. As such, it seems necessary to seek out alternative explanations.

The most obvious interpretation, and in this case the most likely to be correct, if we start from a position of conflict in mid-to-west Devon (as highlighted earlier), is that Ecgberht finalised the conquest of Devon around this time, pushing from the region around Exeter and Crediton towards the Tamar or north towards Launceston.

This may, in this case, be the first time that Cornwall corresponds to its historic boundaries, tying its longer-standing identity into the region that modern audiences will be most familiar with. Between this and the early eighth-century identification of the Cornish as a separate people, it is not entirely without merit to suggest that Cornwall is actually the oldest of the nations that make up the United Kingdom.

While questions around Cornish nationalism are fraught with both emotional and political stakes, it is certainly true that the Cornish as a people originate from outside the English state, and in this regard have as much claim to a national identity as the Welsh or Scots. The counter-argument to this, that Cornwall was absorbed by the English state, could also be made about those two nations, albeit on very different timelines.

Certainly in the early ninth century Cornwall is being referred to, by its own people, by a name we would recognise (Cerniu) while the concept of a singular English state is still not fully formed. Even at the height of his power, Ecgberht is not 'King of the English' – he is instead still King of Wessex, extracting tribute and acquiescence from those beneath him.

The same is true of Wales, where the many small kingdoms will not start formulating a singular shared identity – that of the 'folk' or Cymru – until the tenth century at the earliest.

Returning to Ecgberht and his exploits in Cornwall, the idea of a wholesale conquest is undercut in 825 when, in the same entry describing his victory at Ellandun, a fight is recorded between the men of Devon and the Cornish at Gafulford.

Gafulford was at one time thought to be Camelford in Cornwall; however, this is too far west to be taken seriously and for the most part seems to have been arrived at without considerable supporting evidence. More recent works, such as Higham [2008], have instead looked towards Galford on the northern section of the border between Devon and Cornwall, which seems to have the much stronger claim based on its location along the traditional border and the obvious place-name evolution.

Further, suggestions that Gafulford may translate to something like 'Tax-Ford' also seem to be eminently sensible.

We know that most overland traffic into Cornwall would have had to travel through the northern part of the country; the Tamar Valley and estuary would have been too slow to navigate, even with any ferries that may have been maintained at the time, and so was best avoided. We also see the highest density of English place names in this region of Cornwall, suggesting that it was the area most connected to Wessex.

Further, Launceston's original Cornish name is Dun Heved, 'Dun' being a place-name element relating to a fortified settlement or castle, suggesting that the site was an important guarding point – which makes sense if there was indeed a significant amount of trade and traffic in the region.

Interestingly, Launceston, despite the –ton suffix so typical of Anglo-Saxon settlement, is itself a corruption of a different Cornish place name, Lannsteven, after the church of St Stephen. Of course, the fact it eventually took the 'ton' element is almost certainly to do with growing Anglo-Saxon settlement and interaction in the region.

What remains unknown is who the victor was in this conflict, although, as is typical of many such ambiguous entries, it is often assumed to be the Saxon forces. This was perhaps first noted by John of Worcester in his *Chronicon ex Chronis*, a sort of continuation and adaptation of the *Anglo-Saxon Chronicle* but with a wider scope. The entry in the *Chronicon* for this year reads slightly differently: 'The Britons were defeated at a place called Gavulford by the men of Devonshire.'

While the *Chronicle* is largely thought to have been composed at least somewhat contemporaneously to events, although much of the work of bringing it together is actually undertaken during Alfred the Great's reign, the *Chronicon* is very much a work of the twelfth century. Additionally, the similarity between the entries makes it clear that John, or an accomplice, is working from the *Chronicle* and has chosen to make an alteration to fit his own view.

In fact, there is reason to suspect that the battle may not have gone nearly so well for the men of Devon, and we find it in a pair of charters issued by Ecgberht. Both of the charters [Sawyer, S272 and S273] begin with the same phrase:

Principium autem huius scedulæ scriptum est in hoste quando Egbertus rex Geuuissorum movet contra Brittones ubi dicitur Creodantreow.

> The beginning of this document was written in the army when Egbert,
> king of the Gewisse, advanced against the Britons at the place called
> Creodantreow (Crediton).

As has already been noted, the entry in the *Chronicle* describing the battle of
Gafulford is the same entry for the larger and more notable Ellandun. It has
been suggested that Ellandun, which was fought close to Swindon, was the
result of a Mercian invasion prompted by Ecgberht fighting against the Britons
in the west.

However, given that there is no royal army mentioned in the *Chronicle*, only
the 'men of Devon', it perhaps is more likely that the opposite is true.

As has been noted, Mercia was the dominant power of the eighth century
in mainland Britain. It had also made enemies of Ecgberht at a very young
age. Confronting and defeating Mercia would have been high on his priorities
as king while he went about the business of expanding and consolidating his
power. Chances are he had been planning a battle like Ellandun for years, and
had been mobilising his forces over the course of 825 to see it done.

The proposed battlefield for Ellandun is right in the borderlands between
Wessex and Mercia. If the Mercians had really attacked Wessex while the royal
forces were distracted, it would be assumed that they would have penetrated
much further towards Winchester, the capital, or at least attempted to pillage
some of the nearby rich towns while they were unchallenged. Equally, we
might expect to see some mention in the *Chronicle* of a battle with the local
forces – there is none.

If we consider, instead, that the Cornish, likely still very aware of events
in Devon and beyond, discover that Ecgberht has moved his most powerful
forces far away to the north and east, with only ten years having passed from
Ecgberht's harrying it is likely they would be eager to reclaim territory that
had been recently lost.

This would seem to be supported by the charters themselves. Firstly, the
mention of Crediton as the site of the charters is significant. This was, as
discussed previously, close to the pre-815 border between the Britons and
Wessex, and as such would be an ideal area to prepare to confront Briton
forces in west Devon.

Additionally, there is the dating of the charters. Both charters are noted as
being raised in late summer. In the Early Medieval period the campaigning
season ran essentially over the summer months, with the lower-level freeman
who made up the forces outside the professional warriors needing to return
home ahead of the harvest, as Harold Godwinson found, much to his detri-

ment, at Hastings. This does contrast with a traditional date of September for Ellandun, but that dating doesn't appear in the original sources.

This suggests that the confrontation with the Britons is happening at the end of the season, not the start. Given what we know about Ecgberht's rapid consolidation of power in the aftermath of Ellandun, it is not unreasonable to think that Crediton, at the very far west of his kingdom, was probably the last place he wanted to be with his army, and this suggests in itself that the fight at Gafulford was a defeat for the local Wessex forces which had let the Cornish back into western Devon, a situation Ecgberht could not allow to go unchallenged if he hoped to maintain his hard-won place at the very top.

If this is the way the scenario played out, as the evidence seems to allude, then it shows that the Cornish, far from being conquered from Tamar to Land's End in 815 as some have suggested, were still able to mount large-scale and effective offensives away from their homelands.

Given Ecgberht's rapid rise in the immediate aftermath of Ellandun, it is, however, unlikely that any Cornish gains survived long, but the absence of any mention of a retaliatory campaign might suggest that the Cornish retreated with their spoils and the previous status quo quietly resumed.

Ecgberht himself would soon find another enemy he'd have to deal with: the Vikings.

8

THE VIKINGS IN CORNWALL: THE CORNISH–NORSE RELATIONSHIP AND HINGSTON DOWN

The raid at Lindisfarne in 793 is often cited as the starting point for the Viking Age in Britain, but in reality this is something of an artificial delineation. More recent studies have confirmed a Scandinavian presence in Britain prior to this date (there was even an earlier attack in 789 in Dorset) and there certainly was no immediate rush of Norsemen arriving immediately afterwards.

Instead, mentions of raids and 'pirates' start to increase from this point onwards, building towards the arrival of the Great Heathen Army in the later part of the ninth century.

In Wessex, the first mention of this new threat comes a short time after Gafulford, in 833, when the *Chronicle* records:

> This year king Egbert fought against the men of thirty-five ships at Charmouth, and there was great slaughter made, and the Danish-men maintained possession of the field. And Herefrith and Wigthun, two bishops, died; and Dudda and Osmod, two ealdormen, died.

Thirty-five ships would have represented a significant force of Viking raiders, probably led by an already somewhat successful warlord. Despite this, it's still somewhat unusual to see a battle where Ecgberht comes off the worse. However, it's difficult to interpret this entry in anything but a negative light for Wessex. In particular, the death of two bishops, whom one would potentially not expect to see on the front lines, suggests that it may have been an even less ordered withdrawal then the *Chronicle* paints.

Such a loss would almost certainly become common knowledge very quickly, most likely reaching the ears of Cornwall's king before too long. Perhaps this is why, two years later, a large fleet (potentially the same fleet) of Viking ships arrived in the Tamar and made an alliance with the Cornish to attack Ecgberht's kingdom, eventually facing his forces at a place called Hingston Down.

As the *Chronicle* relates:

> This year a great hostile fleet came to the West-Welsh, and they united together, and made war upon Egbert king of the West-Saxons. As soon as he heard of it he went thither with an army, and fought against them at Hengeston, and there he put to flight both the Welsh and the Danish-men.

For the Cornish this alliance must have seemed an opportunity too good to pass up. After all, they had been fighting more or less alone for more than a hundred years by this point and Ecgberht in particular had proved to be an implacable foe. The opportunity to join with a potentially already victorious army and exact some revenge was clearly enough even to override any objections they may have held towards the Vikings' pagan faith.

Not that this was the first time the Cornish had met the Vikings; or rather, it would seem to be extremely unlikely for that to be the case. As we have noted at various times, Cornwall's infrastructure was built to support an outward-looking, trade-based economy, and this remained true into the Early Medieval period even as the wider power and wealth of the Western Kingdom declined.

Very early in this period we begin to see Viking artefacts emerge at these coastal sites, such as the Borre-style buckle [PAS record: CORN-EC5F13] found at Hayle, whose earliest potential date sits around 800, raising the intriguing possibility that this was left by one of the first Vikings to visit Cornwall.

Despite the highly coastal nature of settlement, there appear to be very few records of any Viking raids in Cornwall, however, at least until the later part of the tenth century when it is much more closely aligned with Wessex.

Additionally, place-name clustering of English names seems to occur largely in the inland zone, mostly in the region between the Tamar and Lynher rivers, while Cornish place names continue to frequent the coastal zone throughout the period [Preston-Jones and Rose, 1988].

Given this information, and the documented alliance that led to the battle at Hingston Down, it seems likely that relations between at least some Viking fleets and the Kingdom of Cornwall were largely friendly.

The question this raises, of course, is why this should be the case. After all, the arrival of Vikings is largely heralded by tales of raids and destruction even if this is eventually followed by peaceful settlement. In Cornwall we don't appear to have this same pattern, in either the documentary record or the archaeological sources.

It is perhaps unsurprising that the Scandinavian finds in Cornwall are largely Hiberno-Norse in origin, meaning that the Vikings who were arriving and potentially allying with the Cornish had come from Ireland and the Irish Sea. This means the Vikings were following in the path of the previous Irish raiders, traders and settlers who had come before. This may mean that there was some ancestral knowledge or experience in dealing with seaborne raiders that served the natives well, an experience that the Anglo-Saxons, themselves originally the shipborne raiders, had not had time to develop. However, it is unclear exactly what form this could conceivably take. With that said, earthworks such as Tintagel's headland, Dun Heved and the Giant's Hedge were still in place even if they were no longer frequently utilised.

The presence of the *teylu* of both the king and lords of Cornwall, experienced and weathered in long years of conflict with Wessex, would also likely have acted as a deterrent for any sudden aggression. Given that elite sites in Cornwall also tended to be within easy reach of at least some of the coastal settlements, it's likely they were never far away.

Additionally, with the Cornish now isolated on the far west of the peninsula, the north Cornwall coastline greeting the arriving Vikings would not have been conducive to the kind of quick hit-and-run raiding they were used to. While there are frequent small bays and inlets perfect for anchoring safely, they are usually surrounded by extreme rises in the terrain, sometimes entirely hemmed in by cliffs of sandstone or granite.

There are also very few navigable rivers, with the notable exception of the Tamar, though this is of course on the south coast.

The combination of these factors may have limited the appeal of Cornwall as a target, but the bays and inlets mentioned would also not have escaped the notice of early Viking captains. We know at least some raiders worked their way around from the Channel into the Irish Sea and vice versa, journeys that can be treacherous around Cornwall's rugged and stormy coast. Having access to safe harbour would therefore be a significant benefit for these journeys. Of course, it would also be a benefit for raiders wanting to plunder Wessex and then retreat to safety before striking out again.

We actually have evidence of exactly this sort of behaviour, although it was not initially described as such.

In November 1774, a group of miners streaming for tin came across a collection of silver objects and coins that had been hidden near the village of Trewhiddle on the south Cornish coast, about a mile from St Austell. Many of the objects were decorated with zoomorphic patterns incised in the metal and picked out with niello. This style of decoration became known as 'Trewhiddle Style' after the hoard; however, many other contemporary examples are found largely in areas around the Midlands and further north.

There are also objects with potentially Irish origins, such as a brooch as well as the chalice the whole assemblage was found inside. The chalice is thought to be the only Anglo-Saxon silver chalice known from Britain; however, its closest parallel is found in a smaller chalice from Lough Kinale in Ireland [Ryan 1990].

The most mysterious of the objects is called the 'Scourge'; it is a braided rope of silver wire woven through a circular object and left with several dangling ends. Its functionality is unknown, although most theories assume it to have some sort of ceremonial or religious significance that has since been lost. Given the number of unknowns surrounding the object, it is also impossible to say for sure where it came from or what its purpose was.

Finally, there are a number of coins, from both Mercia and Wessex, which date the whole assemblage to some point in the latter half of the ninth century with dates around 870 usually suggested.

The Trewhiddle hoard, as it became known, has traditionally been seen as wealth hidden from Viking raiders. However, this view should be challenged. For one, the location of the hoard in relation to known raiding activity makes it a complete outlier; the closest known camp of the Great Heathen Army (whose activities the suggested date of the hoard line up with) is in Exeter, making burial for safety seem unlikely [Hadley & Richards, 2021].

Other factors which seem to work against a 'hidden for safety' hypothesis are the partial or damaged nature of some of the pieces. The Scourge, for example, may well have been part of some larger item which would help to explain its somewhat mysterious origin and purpose. Additionally, there is a collection of semi-circular items which have been tentatively identified as horn mounts; however, these would usually be expected to be made in a single piece. As such it is possible the examples in the Trewhiddle hoard have been broken down for trade or hacksilver from larger, circular originals. There is also the eclectic nature of the assemblage as a whole. While we have consistently emphasised the trading nature of Early Medieval Cornwall, it seems unlikely that a native person would come into possession of all the items in the hoard without having done significant travelling of their own.

When considering the likely candidates for the hoard owner, then – someone who was well travelled around Wessex, Mercia and the Irish Sea and who,
potentially at least, valued silver by weight rather than strictly minted coins – a
Viking raider has to be considered highly probable.

This is then reinforced by Trewhiddle's close proximity to the sea, as well as
the other signs of Viking habitation in the region which we will discuss shortly.

If the Trewhiddle hoard does represent the career savings of a prolific raider
then it was most likely buried in the expectation of being retrieved shortly
after, and this reinforces the idea that Viking ships were using the Cornish
coastline as a convenient safe harbour on their journeys to attack Wessex, no
doubt with the elicit approval and potentially active support of the native elite
and population.

Why the hoard was never retrieved is another question worth asking, and
again it does not seem likely that a local source for the hoard would have
been able to hide such wealth ahead of a raid or other threat without either
its location becoming common knowledge or being overtaken by the events
they were fleeing from.

As for our hypothetical raider, the tentative date of the hoard in the 870s ties
closely with Alfred the Great's victory at Ethandun. Perhaps the hapless owner
of the treasure was relying on an easy victory of the Wessex king trapped in
the marshes before returning for his takings, and ended up finding much more
than he bargained for.

So, if we accept the Trewhiddle hoard as proof of Viking raiders, not just settlers, operating around Cornwall and in conjunction with local entities, we can
start to see how the alliance that fought at Hingston Down may have been forged.

Given that there was already a large fleet operating around the south-west
coast a few years before the battle, it is not impossible that the same fleet, or
even just vessels from within it, would have taken refuge in Cornwall and
spread news of their victory. The Cornish elite, either a local lord or perhaps
even the king himself, would have potentially reached out to this fleet with
the offer of an alliance. There is a persistent rumour in Cornish history circles
that there was a general 'alliance' with the Danes, but this is highly unlikely in
the early stages of the Viking Age when crews were much more likely to be
small and independent rather than part of the overall army of a king or lord.

However, a specific alliance with the fleet that had already managed to
defeat Ecgberht in combat would seem to be an obvious choice for a Cornish
kingdom still angry over the loss of west Devon and eager to exact revenge on
Ecgberht. Arrangements would then have taken some time, perhaps account-
ing for the delay between the two confrontations, in order not just to organise

a return for the fleet but also to gather, arm and equip the Cornish warriors to support the endeavour.

Of course, Ecgberht himself is unlikely to have been idle over this same timeframe, and certainly (given the result of the battle) it seems he had learnt some lessons from his initial clash with the Vikings.

The battle itself is also sited at Hingston Down, near Gunnislake in Cornwall. However, this seems an unusual location, given that the *Chronicle* describes both the Viking fleet arriving 'among the West Wealas' and the combined forces going on the offensive together.

The most likely site for a significant Viking fleet to actually enter into Cornwall, rather than just anchor off the coast, is the River Tamar (as can be seen by the tenth-century raid that destroys Tavistock Abbey). Sailing up the Tamar would also allow the Cornish forces to meet them easily at the edge of their territory and then push forward into Wessex.

The Cornish Hingston Down is, as one might expect, on the west side of the Tamar and is a few miles away from the river. If the allied force is on the offensive then it seems strange they would choose to meet, or indeed be surprised by, Ecgberht's forces inside of Cornwall itself.

This is even more odd when we consider that Viking raiders, dependent as they were on their ships for mobility, usually took pains to maintain lines of retreat to their ships. If they were anchored in the Tamar, as seems most likely, then the Gunnislake site would mean the Vikings were fighting a battle with a Saxon army between them and their ships. This seems extremely unlikely.

Additionally, if Ecgberht had so successfully outmanoeuvred the Vikings as to cut them off from the ships, we would expect the *Chronicle* to record the burning of the fleet or the taking of significant plunder, as it does in other entries; but there is no mention of that here, only of a battle fought at Hengestdon.

The fixed assumption about the location is particularly odd in this case because, unlike several of the other battles we have discussed, there is another Hingston Down a short distance away that would seem a much better fit. Just outside of Moretonhampstead in Devon there is a spur of high ground known as Hingston Down. This is in central Devon, an area we have already identified as seeing frequent conflict between the Cornish and Saxons.

Significantly, the root words for both Hingston Downs are Hengest Dun, or 'Stallion Hill'; this may well, given the importance of horses to the native Brythonic warrior elite, have a secondary meaning or some kind of military significance, potentially as a gathering place for forces.

The eastern Hingston Down seems the much more plausible location for the battle, particularly given that Ecgberht, according to the *Chronicle* entry, has to gather his army prior to confronting them. This would have given the Cornish-Norse forces time to push further into Devon and, largely the Danes, indulge in a bit of looting.

The battle taking place in Devon would have two significant impacts on our understanding of later events. Firstly, and most significantly, it means that the fighting between Wessex and Cornwall (this is the last noted military confrontation between the two) ends not within Cornwall following a successful invasion, but instead in Devon after the Cornishmen's own efforts have been thrown back.

Secondly, it reinforces that the Cornish remain not just an annoyance to Ecgberht but a potent threat to the western regions of his domain.

Regardless of the specifics, the loss at Hingston Down effectively ends the war between Wessex and Cornwall. It is usually assumed that at this point Cornwall is absorbed into Wessex; however, as we shall see, the reality is much more complicated than that.

Hingston Down also wasn't the end of the Vikings in Cornwall. We continue to see signs of Viking settlement throughout the Early Medieval period; however, the evidence slowly changes from scattered personal objects lost over time, like the belt buckle from Hayle or the sword pommel from Penzance, and becomes more emblematic of a population that is putting down roots in the area.

The clearest examples are found in religious stonework.

Firstly, there is the Cardinham Cross, an Early Medieval Cornish cross with an unusual ring chain decoration along its shaft. This decoration is Norse in origin and the closest parallels to it are all found in Scotland, the Isles and other northerly sites. The Cardinham example is an outlier that suggests someone familiar with the artwork had journeyed south to Cornwall, although whether they were the one who commissioned the cross or simply the one who carved it we cannot be sure. The likely date of its construction is sometime in the tenth century.

Then there are a pair of hogback gravestones, the better known of which is found at Lanivet Churchyard. Hogbacks are not specifically Viking artefacts but rather tend to be indicative of Anglo-Danish or sometimes Hiberno-Norse involvement. They are frequently found in Scotland and Yorkshire and in general are indicative of Scandinavian settlement in an area. The Yorkshire stones are quite closely dated to the tenth century, although in Scotland this extends into the eleventh [*The Corpus of Anglo Saxon Stonework*, 2021].

In terms of appearance, hogbacks are large stone sarcophagi which are decorated in a rough proximity of a great hall shape, including engraved tile patterns on the roof as well as long lines of interlace or knotwork pattern on each flat surface. Most typical hogbacks have large beasts on either end of the 'gable', and this is a feature the Lanivet stone does possess, although they are significantly less pronounced than those found on most typical hogbacks. The patterns of stone carving on the Lanivet example are also interesting in that they combine elements of Hiberno-Norse art with traditional Insular patterns, including knotwork that is most often seen on examples around the Irish Sea, including within Cornwall.

The overall impression we are left with is very similar to the Ogham inscriptions from the start of the period and their transition to honouring people with Latin names. It seems like an incoming population has become closely tied into the fabric of Cornish life while still maintaining some of its own cultural identity.

The other potential hogback is found at St Tudy Church, although this one is not such a clear parallel to northern examples: it has an interesting pattern of wavy lines on its side but is otherwise less decorated overall, and lacks the signature beasts on either end. Despite this, there is very little like it in Cornwall other than the Lanivet stone, and as such a potential link or similar purpose cannot be ignored.

The dating of all these examples to around the tenth century supports continuing Viking, or more accurately Scandinavian, presence in Cornwall past the supposed conquest in 836/8. Given that the construction of stone memorials implies at least some level of settled population, both in order to acquire the wealth needed for their construction and to have a local population for whom the monument will serve as a reminder/focal point to your memory or religious pronouncement, it may well be the case that these represent a continuous population from the first contacts in the ninth century.

Given Dumnonia and Cornwall's long-standing role in Irish Sea trade, a trade that was quickly being dominated by Scandinavian interests over this time period with the construction of cities like Dublin, Wexford and Waterford, it makes sense that we would see increasing numbers of Scandinavian settlers within Cornwall both taking part in this trade and as a result of it.

We can see some evidence of this trade network from later period excavation at both Waterford and Wexford (the cities closest to Cornwall), where significant assemblages of Cornish pottery wares have been found [Wood, 2014]. The assemblages in this case are from the eleventh and twelfth centuries, showing the durability of this trading network even in the face of continuous political change – not only the theoretical absorption of Cornwall into Wessex, but also the Norman invasion.

There is, however, a darker side to this trade that should not be ignored. As well as trading for tin and other precious materials, the Vikings were prolific slave traders and all of the Irish Norse cities were involved in the trade to greater or lesser extents. Eventually Dublin would become the largest slave market in western Europe, with slaves taken in Viking raids shipped as far afield as Iceland and Anatolia [Holm, 1986]. There is reason to suspect that the Cornish elite also played an active role in this trade and profited from it.

By some estimates the average percentage of slaves in England was 10 per cent of the population, rising to 12 per cent in some instances. In Cornwall this figure is 21 per cent [Pelteret, 2001] which suggests slave labour was much more widely used then elsewhere in the country. It has been suggested in the past that this discrepancy is due to an incoming English elite enslaving the native population, pointing to the preponderance of English names freeing slaves in the Bodmin Manumissions. However, as we will cover later, the recent revelations around the identities contained within the manumissions make this scenario seem unlikely.

Instead we have to accept that, likely as part of a wider trading network with their Hiberno-Norse allies, the Cornish were actively engaged in the taking, trading and use of slaves.

We can see cultural memories of this in other sources too, such as the *Exeter Book*, a codex of Anglo-Saxon poetry compiled in Exeter in the late tenth century. As well as containing several relatively well-known Old English poems, including 'The Wanderer and The Seafarer', the *Exeter Book* also contains a number of riddles. While some of these are straightforward brain teasers, and usually include their solutions, others are more longform and two of these are relevant to us now: Riddle 52 and Riddle 72:

RIDDLE 52

I saw two prisoners,
borne into the building
beneath the roof of the hall,
both of them stiff –
they were of a kind,
clasped close together
with binding chains –
one of them held close
by a dark Welsh girl
She wielded them both,
fixed in fetters.

RIDDLE 72

I was little…
   [a few fragmentary lines intervene]
   My sister fed me… often I tugged
at my four dearest brothers, each of them
uninjured gave me drink once per day
heavily through a hole. I thrived with a thrill,
until I was older and lonely left that
to a swarthy herdsman, journeying farther,
   treading paths of the Welsh frontier,
cutting across the moors
bound under a beam.
   I had a ring round my neck,
suffering works of woe
along the way,
my portion of hardship.
   Often the iron harmed
me, sorely in my sides—
I kept silent, never
speaking out to any man,
even if the pricking
was painful to me.

Both of these riddles mention Wealas in relation to slavery, either in possessing slaves or being the region where a slave is taken. Given the book's production in Exeter, the most likely 'Welsh' for this to be referencing are the Cornish. This seems to be reinforced by Riddle 72's reference to crossing moors on the Welsh frontier, as a journey from Exeter to Cornwall would involve crossing or circumnavigating Exmoor, Dartmoor and (potentially) Bodmin Moor, all due to the south-west's unique geological makeup.

This would seem to reinforce the impression that the Cornish were taking an active role within the slave trade. While conflict ends after Hingston Down, this may also hint that there are ongoing slave-taking expeditions in and around western Wessex. Whether these are purely Viking activities, sometimes with the unfortunate captives then taken on to Cornwall, or if the Cornish elite are taking part themselves, is unclear.

Before we move on from Norse involvement in Cornwall and back into the main flow of our study, there is one additional assemblage of items that is worth looking at. The portable antiquities scheme has entries for several stir-rups and other horse fittings dating to the eleventh and late tenth centuries. These are all decorated in a typically Anglo-Scandinavian style and seem to have parallels with finds further north, again in areas of heavy Scandinavian settlement. The fact that so many turn up in Cornwall may potentially tell us two things.

Firstly, it may suggest that the native Cornish, with their longstanding links to the Hiberno-Norse world, may well have enjoyed some measure of benefits from the ascension of Cnut to the throne of England in 1012. Certainly, the number of finds all from a similar date range suggest an increase in the level of portable wealth on casual display.

Secondly, the fact that the finds are all parts of horse tack may be indica-tive that the cultural affinity for horses and riding continued well past the fall of Devon to Wessex. However, it must also be considered that the level of general equestrianism in the upper classes was increasing at the time as fashions and warfare on the Continent drove adaptations in Britain, albeit at a much slower rate.

All in all, the continuing Viking presence in Cornwall should be viewed as one chapter in the much longer story of Irish Sea trade and exchange which encompasses so much of the Western Kingdom's history. Once the Vikings became ensconced within that network it was only natural that they would also become part of the fabric of Cornish life and vice versa.

What their continuing presence can also speak to, however, is that, fol-lowing the cessation of direct confrontations between Wessex and Cornwall with Ecgberht's victory at Hingston Down, Wessex still wasn't in possession of Cornwall in a meaningful way. Certainly, it would seem fair to assume that the Cornish kings were now sub-kings to the King of Wessex; however, as we have seen throughout Wessex's history, the level of independence the sub-kings enjoyed could vary wildly over time and between individuals. So long as they remained in nominal control of a region and population that saw itself as separate from the greater whole, there was always a danger of rebellion or disobedience.

This was the situation with Cornwall that Ecgberht left his descendants on his death in 839, potentially only one year after the victory at Hingston Down.

9

RULED BUT NOT CONQUERED: ADAPTATION AND SURVIVAL OF THE CORNISH IDENTITY

Following his victory at Hingston Down, Ecgberht seems to have had at least some hand in starting Anglo-Saxon settlement in north Cornwall. This potentially could be seen as a measure meant to protect the overland route between Devon and Cornwall so that a breakout, such as that which happened at Gafulford earlier in his rule, would not be repeated.

According to the records of Sherborne, he endowed the Church with holdings in Maker, 'Kelk' and 'Ros'. Both Kelk and Ros are more difficult to identify, although it is likely that Kelk relates to Kilkhampton (the English suffix becoming added as settlers arrived) in north Cornwall, reinforcing his interests there [Finberg, 1953]. Maker is obviously at the very far south of the border, just over the Tamar from Devon. However, it is likely in this case that either Ecgberht, or the Sherborne scribes, were attempting to reassert the claim of the Church over the parcel of land granted by King Geraint. Given the collapse of Dumnonia and the fierce fighting that followed, it seems extremely likely that any direct control of the site had long reverted to more local control. It may well be, with this in mind, that the estate at Ros relates to Rame Head close to Maker.

It would be tempting to see the grants at Maker as another response to learned experience, hopefully placing friendly eyes and ears at the mouth of the Tamar to warn of any new Viking fleets entering the river. This very southern outpost would perhaps have felt somewhat lonely, though in truth it was likely manned and managed by local Cornish people. The place-name evidence we have overwhelmingly supports a clustering of immigration in the northern half of the border region, with almost no Anglo-Saxon incursion further west than the River Lynher, itself only a short distance inland from the border at the Tamar.

If we compare place-name evidence for the northernmost 'Hundred' of Cornwall, Stradneth, with the easternmost Hundred of Ryslegh, this pattern is made extremely clear. In Stradneth up to 90 per cent of the place names are either English or have English place name components in them, either a prefix or a suffix, while the density of English place names varies widely across Ryslegh, from as little as 40 per cent in the southernmost section up to 60 per cent in the central body of the region. However, the vast majority of the area is in the lower bracket for percentages [Finberg, 1953].

Of note is that this place-name evidence comes to us largely from modern sources, albeit with some items like the Domesday Book able to corroborate the names and their evolution. As such it represents the sum total of Saxon occupation throughout the remaining 200 or so years prior to the Norman conquest. The strong clustering in the northern area, combined with the previously noted tendency to avoid the coastal settlements, shows that the increasing population of Anglo-Saxons, or English speakers at any rate, were still very much on the outside of Cornish life and power.

One area where unity seems to have proceeded a little more smoothly is in the ecclesiastical realm, with the Bishop of Cornwall, Kenstec, professing obedience to Canterbury sometime between 830 and 874. Additionally the Welsh priest Asser, writing in his biography of King Alfred the Great, states that Alfred passed the control of the Cornish Church to him:

> For in the course of time he unexpectedly gave me Exeter, with the whole diocese which belonged to him in Wessex and in Cornwall, besides gifts every day without number of every kind of worldly wealth; these it would be too long to enumerate here, lest it should weary my readers.

However, when Edward the Elder created the Bishopric of Crediton, he included a stipend in order to support the bishop regularly visiting Cornwall to correct Cornish practices [Charles-Edwards, 2015] as the source puts it: 'For previously they resisted the truth as much as they could and did not obey papal decrees.'

It seems clear from this that the old contentions regarding local Church practice were still going on. Given that both Bede and Aldhelm seemed

particularly concerned with the calculation of Easter, and the singular importance of this date to the Early Medieval Church, it is probable that in this, at
least, they were now in communion with the wider Church but that perhaps
they continued other practices which the wider Church had abandoned or
frowned upon. It's difficult to say with any certainty what these disagreements
or 'errors' were; however, the tonsure is likely to be amongst them and potentially differences in monastic life and rules.

It may also be that Asser's control of the Cornish Church was only ever
nominal at best. As we have seen, there is little to suggest that he was able to
stamp an orthodoxy upon the reluctant Cornish clergy and there is reason to
believe that Alfred's ability to give that control was also extremely limited.

In the period following Ecgberht's death, his son Athelwulf ascended the
throne. Although he was historically viewed as a lesser king, he was able to
defeat Viking raiders in battle at Aclea in 851:

> three and a half hundred ships came into the mouth of the Thames and
> stormed Canterbury and London and put to flight Beorhtwulf, King of
> Mercia with his army, and then went south over the Thames into Surrey and
> King Æthelwulf and his son Æthelbald with the West Saxon army fought
> against them at Aclea, and there made the greatest slaughter of a heathen
> raiding-army that we have heard tell of up to the present day, and there took
> the victory.

He also seems to reorganise Wessex, and helps to stabilise the gains in southern
England that his father had won. In regards to Cornwall, though, there are very
few recorded interactions during Aethelwulf's reign. He does issue charters
granting land in western Devon, including in the South Hams [S298] and in
Halstock [S290] which serves to confirm that the Tamar is now the effective
border between the two realms even if it has not been proclaimed as such.

Given the fighting in western Devon in the years of Ecgberht's reign, it is
conceivable that Athelwulf sought to improve his hold on this region rather
than attempting to gain greater control of the sub-kingdom that Cornwall
had become.

This also seems to be reflected in the growth of tin mining on Dartmoor,
which increases rapidly over the ninth century [Meharg et al., 2012]. It
is possible that whatever accommodation or peace that was negotiated in
Ecbert's time had at least some components about the continued support
for mining and access to the tin trade. As covered previously, tin mining is
a highly specialised industry and it is unlikely that the Saxons would have

had their own expertise to bring to bear, so they would, at least initially, have still been reliant upon local miners. Probably these mining families would have over time mixed with incoming Saxons and passed on their knowledge; however, the craft itself retained a sort of isolated prestige as the establishment of the Stannary Laws and Parliaments in Devon and Cornwall in the Middle Ages makes clear.

While control of Cornwall seems to remain with the local royal line rather than in the household of Wessex, it does seem that Athelwulf believes it safe enough to allow his youngest son to take a journey there on a hunting expedition. As Asser records in his life of Alfred:

> On a certain occasion it had come to pass by the divine will that when he had gone to Cornwall on a hunting expedition, and had turned out of the road to pray in a certain church in which rests Saint Gueriir [and now also St Neot reposes there], he had of his own accord prostrated himself for a long time in silent prayer—since from childhood he had been a frequent visitor of holy places for prayer and the giving of alms—and there he besought the mercy of the Lord that, in his boundless clemency, Almighty God would exchange the torments of the malady which then afflicted him for some other lighter disease.

Cornwall here is identified as a separate region, so it does seem that Alfred is likely journeying in the lands controlled by the Britons. The fact that he was able to do so unmolested suggests that the Cornish kings and their lords, even if not wholly pacified, were no longer eager for an armed conflict with Wessex. This may particularly be true with Athelwulf being in a powerful military position, able to drive off raids from the Cornishmen's former allies amongst the Viking raiding fleets.

On Athelwulf's eventual death, his sons each become king for only a short time. By now the Great Heathen Army of the Vikings is rampaging through Anglo-Saxon England. Unfortunately, a series of West Saxon Kings meet their ends, until Athelwulfs youngest son, Alfred, is acclaimed king in 871.

It should be considered here that a few years after Alfred's coronation, in 875, the *Welsh Annals* have the following entry: 'Dungarth king of Cernyw ‡that is of the Cornish was drowned.'

Dungarth has popularly been linked to the Doniert commemorated on King Doniert's stone in the village of St Cleer. The inscribed stone there includes an inscription: 'Doniert has asked [for this to be made] for his soul['s sake']' (translation taken from English Heritage).

While he is the last documented King of Cornwall that we know of, there are significant gaps in the royal record prior to his death as well, so it should not be taken as fact that he is the last of the semi-independent client kings of Cornwall. For one thing, the fact that the stone was raised to commemorate him strongly suggests there was at least some family left after him to oversee the memorial's construction. As we will see, very little in Alfred's later actions suggests his control of Cornwall was any more firm than that of his father.

While much could be written, and much has been, about Alfred's reign and his wars with the Vikings, there are only some elements of it that are of immediate concern to us.

Principally we should acknowledge that, for most of his early reign, Alfred's immediate concern was events to the north and east of his kingdom where the Great Heathen Army was conquering and plundering much of the established Anglo-Saxon order.

The Viking forces had not only killed his brothers, but by now were tearing their way through the Anglo-Saxon kingdoms of Northumbria, East Anglia and Mercia, subjucating the first two and dividing the third in half, with the greater proportion under Danish control. In such an environment, where it seemed very likely that all of Saxon England may have been wiped out in the near future, Alfred simply would not have had much time to spend attending to the work needed to bring closer unity between Wessex and Cornwall.

The fact that the fighting had ended in Devon and Saxon settlement was limited to the north-east would have left the local elites still in a strong position to govern their areas without the interference of Wessex. To complete the transition of power, Alfred, or another King of Wessex, would need to either forcefully replace that elite or entice them to tie themselves to Wessex voluntarily.

The first option would seem intensely unappealing in an environment where there were already Viking invaders hammering at the door. Not only would it mean diverting forces from the defence of Wessex and sending them on a campaign that they might not necessarily win (the landscape of Eastern Cornwall, particularly in the early Medieval period, would not have been a friendly one, for an unfamiliar army to cross), but it would also risk pushing the Cornish to once again directly throw their lot in with the Vikings. While there is no guarantee that the Cornish elite would survive the latter option, it would become much more appealing if they were being militarily threatened by Wessex once again.

At the same time, bringing the Cornish onside diplomatically would require time and effort that most likely could not be spared in the face of the pressing conflict with the Danes.

The Cornish, for their part, seem to remain neutral in the vast conflict raging to the east. As we have noted previously, we continue to see Viking artefacts in Cornwall well past 838, with the Trewhiddle hoard dating very closely to the peak of Alfred's fighting with the Danes in the 870s. The number of artefacts, the likelihood of Trewhiddle being a Viking treasure and the lack of recorded raids in Cornwall even while other attacks occur in Devon and Somerset, all strongly suggest that the Cornish were still on somewhat friendly terms with at least some of the Viking raiders now frequenting both the Channel and the Irish Sea.

At the same time, it doesn't seem that the Cornish are in any hurry to return to a military confrontation with Wessex.

We can see this most clearly when Alfred faces defeat in the winter of 878. As the *Chronicle* records:

> This year about mid-winter, after twelfth-night, the Danish army stole out to Chippenham, and rode over the land of the West-Saxons; where they settled, and drove many of the people over sea; and of the rest the greatest part they rode down, and subdued to their will; – all but Alfred the King. He, with a little band, uneasily sought the woods and fastnesses of the moors. And in the winter of this same year the brother of Ingwar and Healfden landed in Wessex, in Devonshire, with three and twenty ships, and there was he slain, and eight hundred men with him, and forty of his army.
>
> There also was taken the war-flag, which they called the raven. In the Easter of this year King Alfred with his little force raised a work at Athelney; from which he assailed the army, assisted by that part of Somersetshire which was closest to it.

Not only is Wessex overrun and Alfred isolated at this point, but the fighting also reaches Devon. If there was ever a moment for the Cornish to go on the offensive against Wessex, as they had done only some forty years previously, then this was almost certainly it. However, there is no mention of fighting further west and neither the *Chronicle* nor Asser ever mentions much happening in Cornwall at this time.

The temptation was almost certainly there, particularly if we look closer at the fighting in Devon. Asser provides more details then the *Chronicle*, although not every scholar agrees that they are describing the same events, writing:

In that same year the brother of Inwar and Halfdene, with twenty-three ships, came, after many massacres of the Christians, from Dyfed, where he had wintered, and sailed to Devon, where with twelve hundred others he met with a miserable death, being slain, while committing his misdeeds, by the king's thanes, before the fortress of Cynwit, in which many of the king's thanes, with their followers, had shut themselves up for safety.

The heathen, seeing that the fortress was unprepared and altogether unfortified, except that it merely had fortifications after our manner, determined not to assault it, because that place is rendered secure by its position on all sides except the eastern, as I myself have seen, but began to besiege it, thinking that those men would soon surrender from famine, thirst, and the blockade, since there is no water close to the fortress.

But the result did not fall out as they expected; for the Christians, before they began at all to suffer from such want, being inspired by Heaven, and judging it much better to gain either victory or death, sallied out suddenly upon the heathen at daybreak, and from the first cut them down in great numbers, slaying also their king, so that few escaped to their ships.

The brother is usually assumed to be Ubbe, although there is much that isn't clear about his movements if that is the case. Given the little information we do have to go on, particularly that the fleet overwintered in Dyfed which at the time was the principality in the far south-west region of Wales, it seems likely that the fleet may have been made up of Vikings active in the Irish Sea rather than fresh arrivals from Denmark.

This makes the lack of Cornish support for their attack even more striking, as we have already demonstrated the continuing close contacts between Cornwall and the Hiberno-Norse settlements in Ireland. It seems unlikely that they would have been completely unaware of such a large force active in the Irish Sea.

Of course, there is also the possibility that the Ealdorman of Devon and his men moved to fortify Cynwit and engage the fleet precisely to stop them continuing further south-west and into Cornwall. However, this seems unlikely; given the proximity of Countisbury Hill to the border with Somerset it is likely that the Danes were instead hoping to cut off Alfred and his followers in the marshes from any support that the men of Devon could offer.

If they had designs on retaking the lands lost in Devon, or even to drive out the West Saxons settled in north-east Cornwall, it would appear that this was the moment. The complete lack of evidence showcasing any fighting, either against Vikings or against Wessex, seems to support a neutral stance by the

Cornish. They were biding their time and making sure they had no enemies in either camp so that, regardless of who won in the clash between Dane and Saxon, they might still have Cornwall safe and secure.

This pragmatism would serve them well, particularly once Alfred defeated the Danes at Ethandun and began to reorganise Wessex to improve its ability to repel future aggression and, eventually, take the offensive against the Danes in order to establish a kingdom of the English, and so achieve his great ambition.

It's from this period that we have the clearest evidence that Alfred did not believe Cornwall to be part of his holdings. Or at least, he did not believe it to be defensible or easily taxable.

This evidence comes from the *Burghal Hildage*, a list of all the burghs (or fortified settlements) that had been constructed by Alfred and his son, Edward the Elder, in Wessex and Mercia as it stood at the start of the tenth century.

There is not a single burgh in Cornwall, despite its alliance with the Danes in 838. If Wessex was in control of the region, as is often assumed, you would assume that Alfred would seek to protect it, at least in the regions around the Tamar Valley where longships could easily navigate inland. Instead, the most western of the burghs is at Lydford, around 10 miles from the Tamar and the border with Cornwall.

Interestingly, the *Hildage* lists the lands which Lydford owns in order to support and sustain itself as 150 hides. This is the smallest amount of any of the burghs other than Southampton, which is also listed as 150 [Hill,1969]. This suggests that Lydford was only able to draw upon a relatively small tax base. Certainly the comparison with Southampton is notable, as Southampton obviously is pressed right against the south coast, physically limiting the amount of land it could call upon. In the same way it would appear Lydford's position, close to a border with a still separate and at least semi-independent Cornwall, limited its ability to raise taxation.

Lydford's position is also interesting. It is, of course, situated fairly close to the Tamar, potentially offering a defence against raiders sailing up the river, but it is also far enough back that this seems unlikely to be its only purpose. The fact that it sits essentially in mid-Devon makes it most useful as a blocking position if one expects an attack from the west. While certainly this could be from Viking raiders using the Tamar, it also perhaps hints that Alfred and his descendants were still not entirely certain of Cornwall's loyalties, making the natural ridge defences at Lydford an ideal spot to fortify.

Indeed, Lydford is not attacked for nearly a century after its construction, and when the attack does come, in 997, it is by Vikings specifically seeking to sack the mint that had been established there by that time rather than being intent on plunder elsewhere. It is not hard to infer, therefore, that the siting at Lydford had more than just Viking raiders in mind.

While the pragmatic gamble of the Cornish certainly goes some way to explaining the lack of conflict between Wessex and Cornwall in this time period, it perhaps is unfair to completely discount the hand of Alfred in it as well.

Alfred's vision of a single 'kingdom of the English' was, without doubt, his strongest motivator in the years following Ethandun and the reorganisation of Wessex. But it was not his only goal or indeed his only method of achieving success. He also was a fervently devout Christian who saw value in the Church as an instrument both of God's will and of political expediency.

This perhaps explains his 'gift' of the Cornish Church to Asser. He may even have hoped that a Welsh bishop would have more success in pulling the erstwhile reluctant Briton clergy into closer accommodation with the Saxon Church. As noted, it seems he was incorrect in this assumption, and that is perhaps unsurprising, given, as noted earlier in this text, that the Cornish were culturally less similar to their Welsh cousins than they were to other Celtic peoples from the Continent. This situation is unlikely to have been improved by the physical separation between the groups in the time since.

Still, the increasing evidence for closer ties between Cornwall's Church and that of the West Saxons shows that these early pushes were at least bearing some modest success. It is possible that this growing closeness worked to check any potential pushes for more aggressive actions against Wessex during the latter half of the ninth century.

In fact, upon Asser's death in the tenth century the south-west Church was reorganised with a new bishopric established in Crediton to oversee Devon and Cornwall. However, as noted previously, there were still divisions between the two.

Alfred is also an active diplomat in Wales. Asser records that several of the southern Welsh princes swore him allegiance even relatively early in his reign:

At that time, and long before, all the countries in South Wales belonged to King Alfred, and still belong to him. For instance, King Hemeid, with all the inhabitants of the region of Dyfed, restrained by the violence of the six sons of Rhodri, had submitted to the dominion of the king.

Howel also, son of Ris, King of Glywyssing, and Brochmail and Fernmail, sons of Mouric, kings of Gwent, compelled by the violence and tyranny of Ealdorman Æthelred and of the Mercians, of their own accord sought out the same king, that they might enjoy rule and protection from him against their enemies.

> Helised, also, son of Teudubr, King of Brecknock, compelled by the vio-
> lence of the same sons of Rhodri, of his own accord sought the lordship
> of the aforesaid king; and Anarawd, son of Rhodri, with his brothers, at
> length abandoning the friendship of the Northumbrians, from whom he
> had received no good, but rather harm, came into King Alfred's presence, and
> eagerly sought his friendship

These relations largely seem to be oaths of fealty, with Alfred acting as an over-
king while the Welsh rulers retained their lands and title in exchange for agreeing
to support and obey Alfred. It is unclear how far that support went in practical
terms, but certainly, according to Asser, he continued to be an active diplomat:

> He bestowed alms and largesses both on natives and on foreigners of all
> countries; was most affable and agreeable to all; and was skilful in the inves-
> tigation of things unknown. Many Franks, Frisians, Gauls, heathen, Welsh,
> Irish, and Bretons, noble and simple, submitted voluntarily to his dominion;
> and all of them, according to their worthiness, he ruled, loved, honored, and
> enriched with money and power.

The image we are left with, at least from Asser, is that Alfred sought to establish
a metropolitan court similar to that his grandfather may have encountered
in Frankia with Charlemagne, bringing together Christian peoples from all
corners of Britain (and, notably, Brittany) under his banner. While Asser is
obviously writing a hagiography here rather than a more passive history, it
is worth noting that this 'hearts and minds' approach certainly seems to be
something Alfred's descendants both understand and embrace. It is arguably
the greatest tool his grandson, Aethelstan, will deploy on his way to being Rex
Totius Britanniae, as we will see a little later on.

Certainly, Alfred seems to become something of a magnet for learned
figures from around the British Isles. One of the few sources to mention
Cornwall in his reign is an entry in the *Anglo-Saxon Chronicle* for 891 which
illustrates this:

> And three Scots came to king Alfred in a boat without any oars from Ireland,
> whence they had stolen away, because they desired for the love of God to
> be in a state of pilgrimage, they recked not where. The boat in which they
> came was made of two hides and a half; and they took with them provisions
> sufficient for seven days; and then about the seventh day they came on shore
> in Cornwall, and soon after went to king Alfred. Thus they were named:

Dubslane, and Macbeth, and Maelinmun. And Swinney, the best teacher among the Scots, died.

The other interesting thing about this entry is that Cornwall is again mentioned separately from Wessex. While we do see some regional mentions throughout the *Chronicle*, it normally serves a specific purpose. The fact that the three monks journey onwards from Cornwall to Alfred, and that they had not landed where they hoped, suggests that Cornwall at this point was still considered separate enough to distinguish it from Wessex as a whole.

It may also give us some hint of how Alfred dealt with Cornwall. He may well have been active, not militarily, but in extending a hand of friendship to both the Church and important families and nobles in Cornwall in order to bring them into his influence.

Given the level of success he seems to enjoy in southern Wales, there is nothing to say he was not able to employ the same tactics, including leaving a local elite in place, in Cornwall. However, it is notable that Asser does not mention any specific supplication of the Cornish or their leaders – this may mean that the neutrality we have documented earlier was more firmly established.

Of particular interest is the way the southern Welsh mostly submit due to pressures from their fellow Welsh leaders. The lack of any mention of the Cornish appealing to Alfred for protection again raises many questions about whether they were particularly worried by the Vikings roving in the Irish Sea, or indeed felt the need to attend to the King of Wessex with any urgency.

Upon Alfred's death he seems to control at least some lands in Cornwall directly, leaving Edward the Elder lands in north Cornwall: 'These lands at Straetneat on Triconshire.'

This is usually interpreted as Stratton in the historic Hundred of Trigg. Triconshire is the 'land of three warbands' mentioned earlier in a saint's story. Additionally, he left his youngest son Aethelweard: 'Liwtune and the lands belonging thereto, that is, all that I have among the West-Welsh except Trigg.'

Liwtune is traditionally cited as Lifton in Devon [Finberg, 1953], which was potentially the site of a temporary burgh closer to the Cornish border [Hill, 1969]. It's interesting that only the lands at Stratton are definitely within Cornwall. Lifton is the only named area he passes to Athelweard, the interpretation of him holding lands in Cornwall relying largely on the latter half of the line: 'all that I have among the West-Welsh'. However, when we take a longer look at the history of Wessex in Devon, and in particular western Devon, it could well be that the majority of the population in the region were still Briton or at least came from Briton families.

As such, it seems this reinforces the view that only north Cornwall sees particularly strong Saxon settlement, and potentially Stratton is the only royal estate within Cornwall itself. The monastery at Bodmin, or Bosvenna, is however starting to grow in importance around this time, so it's possible that it was among the beneficiaries of grants given out 'to the church' in Alfred's will, as he was known to frequently give alms to churches outside of Wessex, potentially as part of his diplomatic campaigns as outlined earlier.

With Alfred gone it fell to his son, Edward, and his daughter Athelflaed, 'Lady of the Mercians', to push back the Danes and start the work of building England as we would come to understand it.

Edward suffers somewhat from a bad press, largely because very few primary sources survive from during his reign. This also makes understanding any actions he may have taken in Cornwall even more difficult than with Alfred.

From what little does survive, Edward seems less academic and religiously inclined then his father. William of Malmesbury describes him as 'much inferior to his father in the cultivation of letters'. However, he is apparently 'incomparably more glorious in the power of his rule'.

Certainly, Edward's accomplishments are impressive. Between his efforts and those of his sister, Mercia and East Anglia are completely reclaimed from the Danes and eventually united under the throne of Wessex. This unification is not without some controversy, though it also serves to provide a brief glimpse into the personality of Edward. While his sister was alive she had both the loyalty of the Mercians and rule of the country, maintaining a separate Saxon identity from that of Wessex. On her death she installed her daughter to rule after her (itself an impressive feat in Early Medieval society); however, Edward quickly arranged to remove the girl and bring Mercia's holdings into his own.

It seems clear that Edward was both driven and determined to see his father's vision carried out. A childhood spent on the battlefields of Early Medieval England must have had a serious impact on the growing Edward too, and we can picture a much rougher and more warlike king, ironically probably more in keeping with his ancestors then the more studious Alfred, whose success comes to us unheralded because he did not enjoy the same level of praise from the Church as his father.

It is interesting that the years of Edward's rule, the early half of the tenth century, are also the years when many of the Norse-influenced monuments in Cornwall are being raised. Of course, Edward is a conqueror in many respects, but he also was willing to accept the surrender of settled Danes throughout Mercia and East Anglia; the monuments in Cornwall may well represent one facet of a wider societal acknowledgement that the Danes, in some form or other, were here to stay. Though we talk mostly of the 'Great Heathen Army' as a single rampaging horde, the reality was a much more complicated patchwork of different groups, large and small, and many of these brought their families with them. The erstwhile invaders had put down roots and any attempt now to rip them out would have been a huge undertaking with allegedly limited reward – a fact that Aethelred the Unready would perhaps discover to his cost at the turn of the eleventh century.

In terms of charter evidence, we don't appear to have any issued by Edward granting lands in Cornwall. We can assume he retains control of the estate at Stratton granted to him by Alfred, but beyond this we can only guess how much land may or may not be in royal control.

Diplomatically, Edward still seems to be active in the politics of other regions in Britain, forging alliances with Hywel Dda, Idwal Foel and Clydog. All of them had previously been subject to Athelflaed, and Edward continued to build on these ties much as his father had done [Charles-Edward, 2015]. Hywel Dda in particular was to form an integral part of Athelstan's later efforts to unite all of Britain, so Edward's work here in building these ties (Hywel becomes a frequent witness of Edward's charters) can be seen as absolutely crucial to the later success of his son.

It may be notable that there is no similar presence of a Cornish king witnessing charters during this time. However, as Kevin Halloran [2011] notes, much of the diplomatic pressure on the Welsh, and on other Saxon entities, came from the continuing threat of Viking raiders. This effectively caused a split where the Welsh rulers could either ally themselves with the Vikings, who may prove untrustworthy and who were still unrepentantly heathen, or they could tie themselves to the ascendant Wessex and the Saxons in order to gain support to resist Viking incursions.

Viewed in this context, it may well be that the rulers of Cornwall during this time period were still more in the Viking camp than Edward was entirely comfortable with. However, as we have noted, there seemed to be little desire for a return to armed conflict from the Cornish, and as such Edward may well have chosen to leave well enough alone or to hope his continuing efforts in the Church would bear fruit.

10

ATHELSTAN AND CORNWALL

Athelstan is one of the few Anglo-Saxon kings who is probably better known in Cornwall than he is elsewhere in Britain. That is largely due to the work of William of Malmesbury, whose *Gesta Regnum* provides the following anecdote about his rule:

> Departing thence, he turned towards the Western Britons, who are called the Cornwallish, because, situated in the west of Britain, they are opposite to the extremity of Gaul. Fiercely attacking, he obliged them to retreat from Exeter, which, till that time, they had inhabited with equal privileges with the Angles, fixing the boundary of their province on the other side of the river Tamar, as he had appointed the river Wye to the North Britons. This city then, which he had cleansed by purging it of its contaminated race, he fortified with towers and surrounded with a wall of squared stone. And, though the barren and unfruitful soil can scarcely produce indifferent oats, and frequently only the empty husk without the grain, yet, owing to the magnificence of the city, the opulence of its inhabitants, and the constant resort of strangers, every kind of merchandise is there so abundant that nothing is wanting which can conduce to human comfort. Many noble traces of him are to be seen in that city, as well as in the neighbouring district, which will be better described by the conversation of the natives, than by my narrative.

This is a fine and fiery narrative which has spun many folk tales in its wake. Interestingly, this is a story which is often recited in modern Cornish histories or folk tales, sometimes used as an example of a sort of English ethnic cleansing (an image William's rhetoric does, in fairness, invoke) against the natives.

Whereas we have seen many English sources, both contemporary and modern, exaggerate events in the south-west to their own favour, this is an interesting example of the reverse: English actions being exaggerated to fit a desired Cornish narrative. In some versions Athelstan marches from Exeter throughout Cornwall and conquers the Isles of Scilly beyond [Alexander, 1916]. However, it is also a story with very little basis in fact or sources other than William's writing. In fact, it runs counter to the image of Athelstan most sources paint.

It certainly is true that Athelstan was a successful warrior-king much like his father and grandfather before him. However, he was also one of the most active kings, diplomatically speaking, that Wessex and indeed England would ever see. It was this diplomatic flair that would see him able to claim the title Rex Totius Britanniae, the King of All Britain – a title that so many others may have aspired to but, all relying purely on the sword, none had been able to achieve.

In many ways Athelstan is similar to his great-grandfather, Ecgberht, particularly in the fact that both had a less than promising start to their rule. While Ecgberht was exiled by the designs of Offa of Mercia, Athelstan instead found himself hounded by accusations that his birth was illegitimate. Certainly his father seems to have inherited a somewhat active interest in the opposite sex, taking three wives over the course of his reign (usually not waiting until the previous one was dead but instead 'setting them aside') and fathering many children.

Within Wessex, Athelstan never seems to be popular during his youth, likely due to the machinations of his stepmother, and Edward's second wife, Aefflaed and her family. She, perhaps understandably, acts from a desire to see her children inherit the throne. Instead, Athelstan spent his youth in Mercia in the court of his aunt, Athelflaed, and it is probably here that he learned many of the skills that made him such an effective king. As we have noted previously, Aethelflaed, although not impacting much on Cornwall during her life, was a powerful political player, able to assert her rule over Mercia at a time when a woman wielding such power was practically unheard of.

More than that, she was able to put her daughter in a position to succeed her, which is a remarkable achievement even if it was immediately undermined by her brother.

It is Athelflaed who tends to Alfred's alliances in southern Wales and lays the groundwork for Edward to later build on with powerful figures like Hywel Dda. In fact, it is possible that the Mercian court, placed on the Welsh border as it was, would have had more Brythonic faces in it than Winchester. This potentially left Athelstan with a desire to bring together the Welsh kingdoms with the English rather than attempt conquest. Certainly this seems to be an undertaking he puts considerable time and effort towards, as we shall see.

When Edward eventually died in 924, Athelstan was immediately proclaimed king by the Mercians, most likely due to his long association with that territory as well as the memory of his aunt. However, the Witan of Wessex instead proclaimed his half-brother Aelfweard king. This set the stage for a potentially destructive civil conflict raging in the east. However, Aelfweard died a few weeks later and Athelstan assumed the kingship of both realms.

According to William of Malmesbury, opposition to Athelstan continued to ferment in Wessex, particularly around Winchester, where an otherwise unremarkable nobleman called Alfred apparently plotted to blind Athelstan. While this story may seem far-fetched on the face of it, it's actually attested in a pair of charters which note forfeiture of land by Alfred for conspiracy and include the plot to blind Athelstan. The tale also speaks to an underlying tension between Athelstan and Winchester as the majority of Athelstan's charters in the early years of his reign are undertaken without the Archbishop of Winchester present.

Despite these early trials, Athelstan enters his reign as a king who prefers to use diplomacy rather than the sword where possible. In 925 the *Chronicle* records not just his ascent to the throne of Wessex, but also the following exchange with the Viking king of Northumbria:

925. This year king Edward died, and Athelstan his son succeeded to the kingdom. And St. Dunstan was born and Wulfhelm succeeded to the archbishopric of Canterbury. This year king Athelstan and Sihtric king of the Northhumbrians came together at Tamworth, on the 3d before the Kalends of February; and Athelstan gave him his sister.

Interestingly, a different version of the *Chronicle* records the following the year before:

924. This year king Edward died among the Mercians at Farndon; and very shortly, about sixteen days after this, Aelflward his son died at Oxford; and their bodies lie at Winchester. And Athelstan was chosen king by the Mercians, and consecrated at Kingston. And he gave his sister to Ofsæ [Otho], son of the king of the Old-Saxons.

Both of these entries, although recording the same starting event, Edward's death, give very different impressions of Athelstan's next move. Of course, it is extremely notable that in both versions he gives a sister in marriage to a powerful figure.

Athelstan well understood the value of royal marriages outside of one's own kingdom and his early rule saw a wave of marriages described by Sheila Sharp [1997] as 'a flurry of dynastic bridal activity unequalled again until Queen Victoria's time'. He was particularly keen to establish relations with the Franks, marrying off sisters to the leaders of both Eastern and Western Frankia. Athelstan seems to have viewed the Carolingians as a model to be emulated, even as their dynasty dissolved into splintered factions on the Continent. He was, for example, the first West Saxon king to wear a crown for his coronation, and to be depicted crowned on coinage. Prior to this it was more customary to wear a helmet to display one's role as the defender of the people.

It is interesting, given this wider context and the importance Athelstan clearly placed on his sisters and female relations as dynastic tools, that he would choose to marry one of them to Sihtric, the Viking king of Northumbria. By the beginning of the tenth century, Northumbria stood almost completely alone, sandwiched between the growing power of the rapidly uniting English in the south and an equally emergent Scotland in the north.

It must have seemed obvious to most observers that an independent Northumbria could not long survive in the face of these two expanding powers, and indeed could do little to resist either one without the aid of the other.

As such we might expect Athelstan simply to invade Northumbria; indeed, it seems likely that this is what his father was planning on doing and would have done had he not died at that time. The fact that he instead tries the diplomatic approach speaks to a desire for avoiding conflict if at all possible. It again paints the picture of a king who is happy to achieve rule with the pen rather than the sword; or in this case, by attempting to tie his potential enemies to him so that they can be brought onside. It is difficult to imagine this Athelstan, one willing to marry his own sisters off to foreign kings to ensure peace and friendship, as the sword-wielding nemesis of the Britons that William's tale paints.

However, this tendency for diplomacy, and a willingness to rule through compromise, is a frequent feature of Athelstan's reign. It is likely rooted in the deep Christian faith he professed throughout his life. Like his grandfather, Alfred, Athelstan seems to view the Church both in its role as a political tool but also from a position of genuine belief in its message.

Incidentally, this is probably why the vision of Athelstan presented in the *Chronicle* and other sources is so positive. Unlike Edward, who we have much fewer sources for and who does not seem to have shared his relation's obsession with the godly, Athelstan was an active patron of the Church and sought to bring together learned clerics from across Britain and the Continent at his court. This means the people writing the history, overwhelmingly the clergy, looked upon him favourably in their records.

This actually goes some way towards explaining William of Malmesbury's consistently fawning coverage of Athelstan's reign, and potentially the root of his exaggerations in the case of Exeter's 'cleansing'. The abbey that William attended as a monk, Malmesbury Abbey, was the benefactor of significant grants by Athelstan. Over the course of five charters (S415, S454, S434–436) Athelstan bestows over 160 hides of land on the abbey. This would have been a huge amount of wealth, each hide being sufficient to support a family at the absolute minimum (the actual relation of a hide to a level of wealth is often a confusing and inconsistent subject in Anglo-Saxon Britain).

Interestingly, one of the charters (S415) is one of those including lands forfeited by the plotting Alfred, and contains a summary of the plot. This is most likely where William found the story for inclusion in his chronicle. This does suggest, despite his occasional exaggerations, that he was at least working from first-hand sources in some instances. This is interesting for our purposes, because according to William he had gathered the stories of Athelstan's actions in Exeter by visiting the city itself and speaking to the inhabitants there. Given that we have a likely first-hand source for at least one of his tales, it is perhaps worth accepting the possibility that he did just that.

Viewed in this light, the tale takes on a different quality, for while it may not be accurate, indeed it seems very unlikely to be so, it may instead represent an undertone of resentment or distrust present in medieval Exeter towards the Cornish. Certainly it is not difficult today to imagine bitter words shared between inhabitants of Devon and Cornwall, but perhaps this has a more serious cultural basis.

If we consider again the slavery riddles in the *Exeter Book*, and their likely relations to the Cornish, as well as the events of Gafulford, it may well be that what William is recording here is the result of generations of 'otherness' and distrust between the two sides, intermittently fuelled by armed conflict – though most of this has been gone for centuries by the time of William's writing.

Again, we are given a glimpse into the emergence of Cornwall as it is today; of the feeling that it is both part of a (by now) united English state but also entirely foreign and removed from it.

Stepping away from William and the Church for a moment, there is another aspect of Athelstan's foreign relations that bears looking at. He was an active foster parent for a number of royal scions from across north-west Europe, hosting in his court the princes of Western Francia (also his nephew), Scotland, Norway and Brittany.

His relation with Alan 'Crooked Beard' of Brittany is particularly interesting for our purposes. The Bretons had managed to win their independence as a separate kingdom from the Franks in the middle of the ninth century. However, a period of political unrest was eventually followed by a large-scale invasion and occupation by Norsemen.

As the *Chronicle of Nantes* records:

> Among the nobles who fled for fear for the Danes, Mathuedoi, the count of Poher, put to sea with a great multitude of Bretons, and went to Æthelstan, king of the English, taking with him his son, called Alan, who was afterwards surnamed 'Crooked Beard'. He had had this Alan by the daughter of Alan the Great, duke of the Bretons, and the same Æthelstan, king of England, had lifted him from the holy font. This king had great trust in him because of this friendship and the alliance of this baptism.

Athelstan taking the role of Alan's godfather was a more serious undertaking in the Early Medieval world than it would be today. It was something more akin to a foster father, and certainly Athelstan seems to have taken a significant role in raising Alan.

The Breton state was young and a fairly minor player in European affairs when compared to, for example, the kingdom of West Frankia or Norway where Athelstan's other foster sons came from. Given this, it may seem unusual that Athelstan would take such an interest in its affairs. Yet this is exactly what he did, not only helping to raise young Alan but also giving him ships, men and supplies to help retake his kingdom as laid out by the *Chronicle of Nantes* once again:

> The city of Nantes remained for many years deserted, devastated and overgrown with briars and thorns, until Alan Crooked Beard, grandson of Alan the Great, arose and cast out those Norsemen from the whole region of Brittany and from the river Loire, which was a great support for them. This Alan was brought up from infancy with Athelstan, king of the Anglo-Saxons, and was strong in body and very courageous, and did not care to kill wild boars and bears in the forest with an iron weapon, but with a wooden staff. He collected a few ships and came by the king's permission with those Bretons who were still living there, to revisit Brittany.

For Athelstan to have taken such measures suggests he saw the Bretons and their kingdom to have an importance that their size and political weight would not necessarily merit. Given his drive to become the King of All Britain, it is possible that he believed Brittany to be a potential extension of this realm, one he could hold influence over via his close relationship with its ruling family.

This would fit into his wider work to bring the Welsh kingdoms into closer alignment with the English state, particularly working with Hywel Dda but also the rulers of several smaller Welsh kingdoms who were present at his Winchester court and witnessed several charters, such as S400 and S436. Athelstan, as already noted, was also keen to bring together churchmen from around the British Isles as part of making his court and kingdom a centre of Christian learning.

When all of this is taken together it shows a determination from Athelstan to forge, not just an English kingdom, but a Kingdom of All Britain; an ambition that would probably have seemed impossible even to his grandfather. The fact that he (perhaps) saw Brittany as part of this sphere of influence speaks to both the longstanding ties that remained in place between south-west Britain and the Bretons but also Athelstan's awareness of them.

The crowning achievement of this approach would be seen a year after he had sent his sister north to marry Sihtric, at a small town in the north of the newly minted England. As the *Chronicle* records:

> 926. This year fiery lights appeared in the north part of the heavens. And Sihtric perished: and king Athelstan obtained the kingdom of the North-humbrians. And he ruled all the kings who were in this island: first, Howel king of the West-Welsh; and Constantine king of the Scots; and Owen king of the Monmouth people; and Aldred, son of Ealdulf, of Bambrough: and they confirmed the peace by pledge, and by oaths, at the place which is called Eamot, on the 4th before the Ides of July; and they renounced all idolatry, and after that submitted to him in peace.

It should be pointed out that, following Sihtric's death, Athelstan shows the pragmatic streak which also helped make him such an effective ruler. He doesn't use any further diplomatic overtures to find a new Norse king of Northumbria but simply moves in to fill the power vacuum himself (most likely using his sister's role as queen to give it some justification).

However, the greater achievement here, after all Northumbria's independence was doomed long before Athelstan actually moved in, is the oaths of fealty being paid to Athelstan by the assembled kings of Britain. While both his father and grandfather had worked with, and accepted fealty from, rulers of small Briton states, no one had attempted something so grand as to pull together all the disparate powers in Britain into a single confederation of kingdoms. It's possible that, given the disdain that early English laws, such as those of King Ine, held the native Britons in, no one had actually considered accepting fealty in this way.

For our purposes it is interesting to note that Howel, usually identified as Hywel Dda of Wales, is identified as King of West-Wales. As we have seen earlier in this work, West Wales and the West Welsh usually refers to Cornwall and the Cornish, and its usage here is unusual.

Certainly there is a strong case to be made for this figure to be Hywel Dda. As we have already mentioned, he is a longstanding ally of Wessex and as such his presence would be expected at an event as momentous as Eadmont Bridge. Equally, his footing as first among the kings to be mentioned reflects the reality also seen in the charters he witnesses, where his name is usually the first of the 'Sub Reguli' or sub-kings to appear.

That being said, the usage of West Welsh, an already established phrase with a history that would be known to the *Chronicle* scribes, seems unusual. It has been argued that it is due to Hywel's kingdom, Dheubarth, being on the western edge of Wales. However, that argument seems slightly unusual, especially given the established power dynamic in Wales at the time. While Hywel will, after Eamont Bridge, eventually come to control all of Wales, he was, at the time, only in control of most of the southern portion of modern Wales. The northern portion, Gwynedd, was ruled by his cousin Idwal, who also supported Athelstan and appeared at his court numerous times.

Therefore it seems likely that the more obvious geographic distinction would be northern or southern Wales, and certainly William of Malmesbury talks a great deal about how Athelstan receiving tribute from Gwynedd represents a powerful feat all on its own:

> He compelled the rulers of the northern Welsh, that is, of the North Britons, to meet him at the city of Hereford, and after some opposition to surrender to his power. So that he actually brought to pass what no king before him had even presumed to think of: which was, that they should pay annually by way of tribute, twenty pounds of gold, three hundred of silver, twenty-five thousand oxen, besides as many dogs as he might choose, which from their sagacious scent could discover the retreats and hiding places of wild beasts; and birds, trained to make prey of others in the air.

Again, William is clearly exaggerating for effect here. It's also not immediately clear whether he means Gwynedd or Strathclyde; however, given the location (Hereford), the former seems more likely. We know that Idwal seems to attend Athelstan's court from around this time, witnessing his first charter in 926, so certainly it seems likely this may be the incident to which William is referring. This passage is in the same part of the text as his descriptions of the Cornish being driven from Exeter, so we should treat the military aggrandisement here with the same scepticism; however, the importance William placed on this event does tell us something significant.

From the time of Gildas through much of the Early Medieval period, Gwynedd was frequently the most powerful of the Briton kingdoms and often asserted its power over both its neighbours and the Saxon kingdoms. So Idwal's cooperation with Athelstan would have been a major diplomatic coup indeed.

Eventually their relationship will sour, but the underlying reason appears to be the ambitions of Hywel Dda, not Athelstan himself. In the 940s Idwal will rebel against Athelstan because he fears Hywel is seeking to usurp him. After the war is lost and Idwal is killed, Hywel proceeds to do exactly that, disinheriting Idwal's sons and taking the crown for himself.

However, if we return to the events of Earmont Bridge, the lack of mention of Idwal seems extremely odd. Of course, the *Chronicles* were compiled and copied numerous times, so it is possible that Idwal suffered from some choice editing either within the reign of Hywel or even just beyond, but given William's overzealous recounting of Gwynedd's capitulation it's clear that the kingdom's power still echoed in the cultural memory and, as such, we would expect a record of its surrender to be included for posterity.

As such, the exclusion of Idwal, and the use of West Welsh for Howel, leaves many questions hanging over the *Chronicle's* account of Eadmont Bridge. A number of possible explanations, including Howel simply referring to Hywel Dda as is currently believed, can be proposed when looking at these questions.

The first is that the entry in the *Chronicle* is an incomplete list. The actual meeting at Eadmont Bridge could have been attended by a larger number of kings than is listed (the kings of all Britain, as William writes) and this list was cut down over time. This potentially explains Idwal's exclusion and could explain the use of West Welsh if a Cornish king was also in attendance (potentially even another named Howel) and his suffix was appended to another name.

This isn't as hopeless as it may appear. The meeting at Eadmont is, after all, only fifty years from 875 and Dungarth/Doniert's unfortunate swimming accident. It is entirely possible that the family who raised the stone to his memory could still have been in power in Cornwall.

Which brings us to the other possible scenario: it could well be that the *Chronicle* entry refers to exactly who it says it refers to – that is, a Howel of West Wales or Cornwall. While we might expect Hywel Dda to be at such an event based on his longstanding relationship with the ruling house of Wessex, it could also be that he isn't there for exactly that reason. He has already given his fealty to Athelstan and as such it is not necessary for him to do so again. Meanwhile, the other major rulers who are listed at Eadmont – the kings of Scotland and Strathclyde and the Lord of Bamburgh – are all new vassals to Athelstan whose allegiance hadn't previously been secured.

Would a potential King of Kernow fit this mould? Well, as we have seen, the fighting between Wessex and Cornwall ends in a sort of uneasy allegiance. The Cornish are at once subject to Wessex and yet removed from it. The wars with the Danes in the years since had also left little opportunity for Wessex to assert its control over much more than the very north-eastern corner of the country.

Fealty is also never set in stone in the Early Medieval world. A close parallel may be seen in the Breton experience, where Erispoe and his predecessors consistently rebelled against then rejoined the kingdom of West Frankia, until he and his son eventually secured their independence at the battle of Jengland.

Indeed, we have very little evidence, until Athelstan's reign, of the Cornish becoming particularly more English; unlike their former relations across the Tamar in Devon, who adopt the English language and Saxon patterns of organisation and landholding.

This suggests that, while there can be no doubt that Kernow no longer posed an imminent threat to the stability or power of the emerging English state, it was still not fully integrated into it. Indeed, there may have been no formal agreement over exactly how much control or tribute was to be awarded by one side to the other (or if there was, it may well have lapsed over the long years of the Danish invasion).

As such, it may have been prudent for Athelstan to formally and publicly bring Kernow into his control at Eadmont Bridge. Some level of political realignment would also potentially explain the still-simmering cultural tensions that William recorded during his conversations in Exeter.

Certainly Athelstan was as busy in Cornwall as he was in other regions, and his actions (as elsewhere) seem to rely on diplomatic concessions to a presumably still active Cornish elite in order to win their loyalty.

The most dramatic of these moves was perhaps the re-establishment of a Cornish bishopric, based at St Germans, and the separation of religious jurisdiction in Devon and Cornwall between this new see and the Saxon minster at Crediton. As we have seen, the variation of customs between the Cornish Church and that of Wessex was not only a point of repeated conflict but also, given the repeated overtures by Wessex to resolve it, a key facet of its attempt to dominate the south-western Britons.

In the seventh century it was Aldhelm's religious concerns that set the scene for the invasion of Devon and the sundering of Dumnonia. It also put the first Cornish land (the lands around Maker) into Wessex hands. However, as highlighted by Edward's grant to the Bishop of Crediton, the Cornish Church clung to its own identity. In fact it may, as Olson [1989] suggests, have maintained some measure of its own hierarchy despite the continuing pressure from Wessex and Crediton.

As such, Athelstan's creation of the new bishopric is, in some ways, an acknowledgement of the political reality he inherited. However, by not just accepting this reality but making it official policy, he was able to step away from the failed policies of his predecessors and also make an overture to the native elite.

Viewed in this light, the first bishop, Conan, being a native Cornishman, can be seen as another concession to the local elite. In actual fact the first three bishops, as discussed by Insley [2003], are all either confirmed to be or extremely likely to have been Cornish.

As for what Athelstan, and the kings who followed him, could have gained from the arrangement, we need to look at the Church they were supporting. As Insley points out, the Cornish Church itself not only survived in the face of Wessex's expansion but actually thrived, particularly in terms of ongoing patronage. This means it was not just a powerful institution but also one in control of significant wealth and lands.

This would have made it a powerful and influential voice among the other Cornish nobles, the *teyrns* or chieftains who would have led their *teylus* against Wessex in the conflicts of the eighth and early ninth centuries. By bringing them onto his side, or at least granting them a new legitimacy within the English state, Athelstan may have done a huge amount for his standing amongst that same nobility.

This not only would have been a significant step in securing the western borders of Wessex but, more importantly, it would also serve to improve relations with the Cornish families who still controlled many of the natural tin deposits in England.

Finds like the Praa Sands ingots, an assembly of tin ingots ranging in size from a sliver to a full hemispherical ingot with a cross mark embossed on it, highlight the ongoing tin production and trade that was central to the Cornish economy. The ingots themselves have recently been redated to the mid-ninth century, showing this trade was ongoing even as the Great Heathen Army warred with Alfred [Biek, 1994].

With the Cornish still in only passing compliance with Wessex, it is likely that much of the profit, and potentially taxation, of the tin trade was still escaping the royal coffers – especially given, as discussed, the largely marine nature of the trade. As the demand for bronze products continued to grow, as well as other uses such as solder for statuary decoration, the value of tin would have increased throughout this time. However, the mining and refinement of tin is a highly skilled process and, as such, was difficult to replicate without the expertise of Cornish miners, although the lords of Devon no doubt had attempted to encourage miners on Dartmoor to remain in the county.

The establishment of the new diocese certainly seems to mark a turning point in relations between Cornwall and the English state. From this point on we begin to see a number of charters issued by English rulers to both Cornish institutions, in particular the Church of St Petroc at Bodmin, but also to the diocese at Crediton in what would seem to be recompense for losing the nominal control of, and presumably the tithes that went with, the Cornish Church.

These charters replaced an earlier tradition, described by Wendy Davies [1982] as the 'Latin Celtic Charter', which are best encapsulated by the Llanlawren charter. This is a ninth-century charter, translated by Oliver [2016] from a fifteenth-century copy, which records a grant of land from Maechi who is described as 'comes', essentially a military title which implies he was some sort of warrior or, given he is granting land here, a leader of warriors. He grants the land to St Heldenus, which is assumed to be a religious institution that is otherwise unknown in the period. What is interesting about the Llanlawren charter is that, while it is described as the only 'true Cornish charter' by Padel, it is made with a care of language and specificity of form that implies this was far from an unusual creation. This suggests that the legal tradition of Cornwall was at least as developed as the Saxon tradition and, given the date of the Llanlawren charter in the second quarter of the tenth century, it survived long past the end of hostilities with Wessex. Even the simple act of a Cornish noble supporting a small religious institution on his own speaks strongly of an independence of action and, potentially, longstanding tradition.

This reinforces a Cornish identity that remained much more separate from Wessex than was previously assumed. Rather than being absorbed fully after Hingston Down, the Cornish institutions, both religious and secular, continue in their own traditions and seem to actively resist the efforts of Wessex to enforce change.

This began to change in the early tenth century; while the Llanlawren charter represents a longstanding native tradition it is soon joined by a number of royal charters from Aethelstan granting lands in Devon and Cornwall to his new Cornish bishopric or to the old institution at Crediton. The number of charters and their locations seems to suggest that Aethelstan is attempting to move holdings of the English Church out of Cornwall while simultaneously moving Cornish holdings west of the Tamar. This suggests a level of cooperation with the local Cornish aristocracy and may in fact be the basis for the famous settling of the border [Insley, 2013].

If Aethelstan did move the border officially to the Tamar, it is likely that he was simply reinforcing what had, by that point in the tenth century, become the status quo. While there may still have been Cornish landholders on the eastern side of the Tamar, and indeed the Church at least clearly did hold lands there, it is likely that their actual control or say in the runnings of those lands would have been greatly diminished over the years.

As such, this could be seen as the other side of the compromise that gave renewed life to the Cornish Church.

The diplomatic approach, seen in Cornwall and Wales, certainly seems to have been effective. In the years following Athelstan's rule there are a dozen charters issued by English kings either of land in Cornwall or gifting land to bodies (usually religious institutions) within it.

To see just how effective it may have been on a wider scale, we can actually turn to a Welsh source: a barnstorming tenth-century poem known as the *Armes Prydein*, or 'The Prophecy of Britain'. Written sometime in the mid to late tenth century, the poem is a call to arms, describing how all the Brythonic peoples (and their Viking friends – potentially important given the demonstrated links between Cornwall and the Scandinavian world) would rise up against the Saxon English and throw them back into the sea:

> The contention of men even to Caer Weir (Durham), the dispersion of the Allmyn (English)
> They made great rejoicing after exhaustion,
> And the reconciling of the Cymry and the men of Dublin,
> The Gwyddyl of Iwerdon (Irish), Mona, and Prydyn,
> Cornwall and Clydemen their compact with them.
> …
> That the Allmyn are about to emigrate abroad,
> One after another, breaking afresh upon their race.

The Saxons at anchor on the sea always.

The Cymry venerable until doomsday shall be supreme

The poem is notable for several reasons. Perhaps the most important is the very early use of Cymry to identify the Welsh as a single people rather than a group of disparate principalities. This echoes similar national identities that we have seen being forged in England and Scotland during the tenth century. This effectively completes what we might consider to be the modern map of British identities.

As previously noted, all of these are also predated by the identification of Cornwall and the Cornish, which appears at the start of the eighth century at the very latest.

It's also interesting to note that, while each nation in the coalition is introduced singly, Cymry is used from that point on to refer to the whole group. This seems to indicate, to the poet's mind at least, that all the Brythonic peoples were part of this same singular people, an attitude that is still reflected by organisations such as the International Celtic Congress.

There are parallels to be drawn here between the Welsh poet's viewpoint and that of Athelstan himself. As we have seen, he seems to have gone to great efforts to incorporate Welsh kings, the Cornish Church and even Breton nobility into a power network with himself at the centre.

The *Prydein* is probably written towards the end of Athelstan's reign, or possibly just after his death. This means that, in terms of Welsh politics, it is written at around the peak of Hywel Dda's power. The king had managed to use his links to Athelstan, as well as his own political savvy and manoeuvrings, to bring almost the entirety of Wales under his direct rule. He also continued to support Athelstan's successors and avoid open conflict with the English.

There were still advantages to this approach. For one, it avoided further English expansion into Wales as focus remained largely to the north or towards the shore seeking out Viking raiders.

In such an environment the *Prydein* can be viewed as a direct attack on Hywel's policies, a repudiation towards him (and, by extension, the native Cornish elites and their Breton peers). Additionally, given the rapid arrival of the Vikings back both in the Danelaw and raiding around the coast in the years following Athelstan's death, the poem can be seen as a literal call to action, a demand to seize the opportunity to take back land from the Saxons while they were fighting other foes.

In this regard the poet also seems to be giving voice to an undercurrent of hostility from the Brythonic side, an acknowledgement that, while the rulers of the day may urge integration, it would never be so easy for the common people. It is practically a mirror to the hostility William of Malmesbury recorded on the streets of Exeter so many centuries later.

It should be noted, though, that the very fact the poet, writing in a persuasive style similar to the finest propaganda, felt the need to agitate for an uprising against the English speaks to the effectiveness of the conciliatory approach undertaken by Athelstan and his successors.

We can see the legacy of this in Cornwall, in one of the finest single artefacts from the Early Medieval period in the south-west: the *Bodmin Gospels of St Petroc*, otherwise known as the *Bodmin Manumissions* (although this strictly only refers to certain sections), is one of the most, if not *the* most, important books in Cornish history.

This importance comes from several factors, and it is worth looking at each of these in some detail. Initially, it is worth considering what the *Gospels* tell us about Cornwall and its place in the Early Medieval world during the ninth and tenth centuries. The *Gospels* themselves were produced in Brittany sometime in the late ninth century and then were procured by the Church of St Petroc shortly after. This serves to underline the continuing strong links between Cornwall and Brittany that we have discussed previously. It also highlights that, culturally at least, the Cornish Church still showed a preference for 'Insular' art – that is, the art style predominantly found around the Irish Sea and in Brittany, of which the *Book of Kells* is probably the most extravagant example. This is despite a contemporary style of Anglo-Saxon illumination being developed in Wessex and elsewhere. We have already shown the continued survival of some level of separate Cornish Church even prior to Athelstan's reorganisations, but this stylistic difference marks just another facet of that divide.

There were further artistic flourishes previously present in the *Gospels*, including illuminations of the four Evangelists in a style likely reminiscent of the *Landevennec Gospels*. Unfortunately, these decorations were intentionally removed at some point during the book's life, which is obviously a significant loss for modern historians.

It is also worth noting that the *Gospels* themselves contain examples of writing in Latin, Cornish and Old English. This showcases not only that there were at least some Old English speakers present in Bodmin at the time, but also that native scribes were able to write and understand a number of different languages, which suggests a high degree of learning and cultural exchange.

Moving on from the *Gospels* themselves, there are then the *Manumissions*, referring to the ritualised freeing of slaves in a church in order to reap heavenly rewards, which are perhaps the most famous part of the book. The manumissions are recorded both on their own pages (appended at the end of the *Gospels* themselves) and in the margins of the *Gospels*. They record dozens of names of both slaves and their owners and, as such, offer a vital resource for ethnographers looking for tangible evidence for the longstanding Brythonic Cornish identity we have encountered throughout this work. It has also, in the past, been something of a double-edged sword for those interested in the history of Cornwall and the Cornish and how the relationship between the Cornish and the English developed into its current state.

This is mostly because a majority of the released slaves, potentially as high as 80 per cent, have identifiably Brythonic names, while a majority of those doing the releasing seem to have English or Saxon names. This has previously been taken as proof that the Cornish were a conquered people, subjected to slavery within their own country. However, as we have discussed previously, slavery was a major feature of life around the Irish Sea, to an extent not really seen in the rest of Anglo-Saxon England (although there were certainly slaves present there too). The Cornish had taken an active role in this trade and, as such, seeing a high volume of native slaves should not be surprising in and of itself. As for the English names of the enslavers, thanks to research by Picken [1986] and others we can positively identify at least one of these English names as a Cornishman using an official alias. Wulfsige, the third bishop of the Cornish diocese, is elsewhere identified as Comoere, a more ambiguous, but likely to be Brythonic, name.

The decisive entry, illegible until looked at forensically was: 'This is the name of that woman, Guenenguith, and her son whose name is Morcefres who[m] Bishop Comoere freed on the altar of St Petroc for the redemption of his soul in the presence of these witnesses.'

The dating of the entry, and the title of bishop, ties Comoere closely to Wulfsige.

There are also a further two instances, noted by Charles Insley [2013], where tenth-century charters (S755 and S770) list beneficiaries who use both Cornish and English names. These are Aelfheah Gerent and Wulfnoth Rumoncant, both of whom are the recipients of land from King Edgar. It is also interesting to note that, in each case, they are listed as either faithful vassals or 'His Man' in the charter text. This implies that, not only are these (presumably) native Cornish elites now fully integrated into the apparatus and legal framework of the English state, but they have also come to serve the royal house directly. This suggests that, given the mores of Early Medieval lordship and reciprocal duties, they were likely engaged in some form of military service as well as general fealty to the king.

Returning to the *Gospels*, the dual names of Wulfsige, Aelfheah and Wulfnoth all show that the presence of an English name does not, by the tenth century at least, automatically indicate the presence of an English person. In fact, given the higher levels of involvement the Cornish elite had always had in the slave trade, it would perhaps be safer to assume native elites in most cases, although obviously this will not be a foolproof approach either.

Certainly this seemingly widespread adoption of dual English-Cornish identities seems to underscore a Cornish elite which is tying itself more firmly into the English state, possibly seeing this as the best road for its own advancement. At the same time, both the practices around slavery and the retention of Cornish names suggests this remains just one layer of identity and the older Cornish layer remains very close to the surface.

Finally, we should address the *Gospels'* importance to the Cornish language: the *Gospels* and *Manumissions* contain the earliest examples of written Cornish in the world. Ahe Gospels manuscript also contains a dictionary with words ranging from the mundane to the ecclesiastical; an absolutely vital resource in preserving the legacy of written Cornish into the modern world.

The final legacy from Athelstan's reign in Cornwall is the formal organisation of the Hundreds or *keverang*. These are subdivisions of the country into administrative districts, similar to the Anglo-Saxon Hundreds or the Welsh *cantrefs*. In some sources the word, *keverang*, is translated as 'war host', but this seems to be potentially apocryphal as most modern translations link it more closely to an administrative unit only.

The Cornish Hundreds do bear some differences from their English counterparts and they also survive much longer, eventually forming the basis for the local Cornish militia and army in more recent centuries. Whether these represent an older form of administration that Aethelstan simply made official is harder to tell. Certainly the similarities to the Welsh Cantref would potentially indicate that the Hundreds represent a similar concept. It may also be worth remembering the 'Lord of Three War Hosts' mentioned in earlier centuries, who may well represent an ancient leader of one of these subdivisions.

Following Aethelstan's death, his successors were eventually able to grant lands more widely in Cornwall, moving from the eastern fringes all the way to the Lizard and Land's End. Still, they seem to do so in conjunction with local elites (for example, Edgar's grants to two Cornish nobles) and are somewhat considered in their approach.

In various charters they seem to make reference to some of their holdings lying outside of 'England', providing a tacit admission that Cornwall still maintained a somewhat separate identity from the central English state. Some examples of this can be seen below:

S498 King Edmund I to Athelstan 'Comes' grant of lands in Devon
Edmundus rex Anglorum huiusque provincie Britonum
Edmund King of the English and ruler of this Province of the Britons

S770 King Edgar to Aelfheah Gerent
Eadgar rex Anglorum ceterarumque gentium in circuitu
Edgar King of the English and other nations around them

S832 King Edward the Martyr to Aethelweard 'Comes'
rex Anglorum ceterarumque circumquaque nationum
King of England and of other Nations

While it is inarguable that Cornwall and the Cornish elite were, bit by bit, fully incorporated into the English state so far as legal control and, importantly in the Early Medieval period, military obligation were concerned, these small concessions in legal niceties continue to give hints of the character of Cornwall, the unique Brythonic heritage which it had managed to preserve in the face of increasing pressure from Wessex. The most intriguing entry in the later part of the tenth century comes from Aethelred II, known as the 'Unread' or poorly advised. He issued a charter confirming the grant of lands to Bishop Ealdred of Cornwall and used the following phrase to describe the holdings:

Ealdredi episcopi id est in prouincia Cornubie
Ealdred Bishop in the province of Cornwall

The use of 'province' to describe Cornwall is interesting as it carries with it very specific connotations which are separate from simple ideas of rulership. A province is, usually, a region with its own ruler or government who are subservient to an over-king. This would be most often seen in the earlier Saxon period, when the various kingdoms of the Heptarchy might try to foist this status on their neighbours. Given the lack of information we have about any surviving Cornish royal family, it is difficult to say that this would denote the survival of some kind of under-king; however, it does very clearly speak to the continuing unique identity of Cornwall and how this would eventually be moulded into the Duchy of Cornwall in the Later Medieval period.

Duchies on the Continent, for example Brittany, were often provinces of this type; that is, regions with significant autonomy or unique cultural identities which were nevertheless ruled (sometimes only nominally) by another party.

It's probably worth noting that the late tenth century – this period of closer integration with the English state – also marks one of the only recorded Viking attacks in Cornwall. In 981 the *Chronicle* records: '981. In this year St. Petroc's-stowe [Padstow] was ravaged; and that same year was much harm done everywhere by the sea-coast, as well among the men of Devon as among the Welsh.'

This attack led to the monks of St Petroc's moving the saint's relics and shrine to Bodmin, probably reinforcing the importance of the already fairly wealthy church there as St Petroc was an important figure throughout Cornwall. It is interesting to note here that the *Chronicle* still refers to the Cornish as 'Welsh' (original 'Wealas') or foreigners.

While this is a point we keep returning to, it is worthy of repetition. The continuing 'otherness' of the Cornish is a notable outlier when compared to the Briton inhabitants of other regions the Saxons successfully subdued. Across the whole of England, with the notable exception of place-name elements such as Kent, there is no other group that retains its original Brythonic identity once it is integrated into the English state or one of the smaller Saxon kingdoms. The continuing proof that the Cornish did exactly this is testament not only to the period of open warfare during the eighth and ninth centuries, but also to the eventual negotiated settlements with Ecgberht and then with Athelstan. The Cornish elite, and the people they ruled, bent with the prevailing winds but never broke and as such preserved their identity and language into the modern era, whereas other groups, such as the Durotriges to their east, vanished almost entirely.

Further confirmation of this separate Cornish identity can be seen in the will of King Eadred (died 955) which lists all the southern shires of England but noticeably does not include Cornwall in this list. This indicates that Cornwall still holds a separate identity to a shire, most likely the earlier quoted idea of a 'province' with all the legacy of former kingship it bears with it.

As the tenth century moved into the eleventh, the old Anglo-Saxon order was eventually replaced as Viking raids increased during the reign of Aethelred, until a full-scale invasion arrived led by Sweyn Forkbeard of Denmark and his son, Cnut. Sweyn and Cnut fought a series of engagements with Aethelred and his forces until they had driven him into exile. An entry in the *Chronicle* for 1013 notes:

Then went king Sweyn thence to Wallingford, and so over the Thames westward to Bath, and sat down there with his forces. And Ethelmar the

ealdorman came thither, and the western thanes with him, and they all submitted to Sweyn, and delivered hostages for themselves. And when he had
thus succeeded, then went he northward to his ships; and then all the people
held him for full king.

Simeon of Durham, a twelfth-century monk and chronicler, lists Ethelmar as
Ealdorman of Devon [Stevenson, 1855] which, if correct, would seem to indicate that the western thanes are likely to be the majority of the leaders from
Devon, Cornwall and Somerset. Given the number of charters in Cornwall
listing the recipient as 'Comes', or even just to non-Church figures, we have
to assume that the Cornish nobility were tied militarily to England. That is,
they held their lands on the understanding that they would support the king
or their overlords in times of conflict. As such this submission is very likely to
have included Cornish nobles in its ranks, or at least a delegation thereof.

Not that the peace was to last. Sweyn would pass away shortly after and
Aethelred was called back from exile. However, Cnut arrived soon after and
again managed to set Aethelred to flight. Eventually he entered a conflict with
Edmund Ironside that would see England divided between the south and west
on one side and north and east on the other. In this, as we have noted, he likely
had at least some support from the Cornish nobility, although the majority of
the fighting took place a great distance from the far south-west. There is no
further mention of the western thanes, though, so we cannot be sure of their
presence or absence.

Eventually, Edmund himself dies and Cnut takes the whole of England
for himself, though notably makes no claim on Wales or Scotland which had
previously slipped the control of the English.

There is a persistent rumour, often quoted in historical websites or even at
visitor attractions in Cornwall, that Cnut did not claim Cornwall as part of his
territories; however, in the course of researching this book I have found no
evidence to support the claim.

Cnut takes all the holdings of the English kings as his own, and even has a
Devonshire lord, Brictric, killed upon taking power (presumably as revenge for
the western thanes once more taking up arms), suggesting his power extended
at least as far as the Tamar. As we have noted, the nobility of Cornwall had,
by this point, very closely aligned themselves with England while maintaining elements of their own identity. However, there is nothing to indicate that
anyone was in a position to assert Cornish independence in the face of Cnut's
invasion and even less to support what might have happened to it afterwards
(there is no entry describing a reclaiming of Cornwall after the fact).

In fact, Cnut issued two charters granting land in Cornwall (S951 and S953) which seems to put to rest any notions that he did not consider those lands as part of his domain.

As the Anglo-Saxon period comes towards an end in the mid to late eleventh century, there are two final entries in the *Chronicle* that are of interest to us. Both involve the Godwins, the powerful family of Wessex nobles who would dominate much of the reign of Edward the Confessor before seeing their eldest scion, Harold Godwinson, crowned king during the tumultuous events of 1066.

In 1048, though, Godwin had overplayed his hand and both he and Harold were exiled and stripped of their earldoms:

> And then Odda was appointed earl over Devonshire, and over Somerset, and over Dorset, and over the Welsh. And Algar, the son of Leofric the earl, was appointed to the earldom which Harold before held.

Again we find that the Cornish have retained the 'Wealas' title, even here at the very end of the Anglo-Saxon period. It is particularly interesting given what will follow in the years following 1066. Despite this continuing difference, King Edward is able to dissolve the Cornish Bishopric in 1050 and combine it with the see of Devon into a single diocese based in Devon. Given the importance of Athelstan's formation of the separate Church in achieving unity, it seems clear that by this point the Cornish are fully integrated into the English state, including religiously, whereas this had previously been a continuing sticking point.

In 1052 the other entry which is of interest to us notes:

> This year came Harold, the earl, from Ireland, with 9 ships to the mouth of the Severn, nigh the boundaries of Somerset and Devonshire, and there greatly ravaged; and the people of the land drew together against him, as well from Somerset as from Devonshire; and he put them to flight, and there slew more than thirty good thanes, besides other people: and soon after that he went about Penwithstert [Land's End].

This ravaging was part of Harold's, and previously his father, Godwin's, attempts to force Edward to end their exile by making their absence more painful than their presence had been. However, Harold's ravaging of Devon and Somerset, and presumably at least some parts of Cornwall given the trip around Land's End, would have won him no friends. He, or more accurately his family, would perhaps have cause to regret these actions later on, though that would take some time to bear fruit. For now it does make clear that, while Harold will eventually be instated as Earl of Wessex, he remains a Sussex man (where most of his family's lands were) at heart, with no particular love for Wessex's traditional heartlands.

PART 3

SURVIVING AND THRIVING: CORNISH IDENTITY AND LANGUAGE POST-1066

11

THE NORMAN
CONQUEST IN
CORNWALL: FRIENDS
IN HIGH PLACES?

In the winter of 1065, Edward the Confessor fell ill and the Witan, the Anglo-Saxon body that elected kings when there was no direct heir or (as was the case here) the obvious heir was too young for the role, hurriedly met to await his death. They didn't have to wait long. In January 1066, Edward was dead and the Witan hurriedly voted in Harold Godwinson, the son of the powerful Godwin and erstwhile raider of the south-west coastline, as the new King of England.

Of course, this relatively simple chain of events was powerfully disruptive to all of north-west Europe, eventually resulting in the deaths of two kings and England coming under the rulership of William the Bastard of Normandy, who also got a somewhat more pleasant suffix to his name in the process.

The Norman conquest of England was also the death knell for the Anglo-Saxon ruling class who had arrived in the post-Roman world of the fifth century and had, over the course of centuries, created the large, powerful and, most importantly, rich country of England that so many rulers in 1066 desired to hold. For the Saxons, peasant and noble alike, this was a singly disruptive event. Those at the top, or at least those who survived the slaughter on Senlac Ridge, were largely stripped of their lands, while those at the bottom swapped the longstanding legal protections and reciprocal relations with their lords for the much more restrictive form of feudalism.

However, it is interesting to note that there doesn't seem to be the same level of severe disruption in Cornwall. In actual fact, the post-Norman period can be seen as a high point, at least as far as the production of Cornish writing and materials is concerned.

To understand how the situation may have benefited Cornwall, we need to look at a number of factors: the impact of 1066 on Cornwall itself, the long-standing Cornish relations with the Bretons, and what the Domesday Book can tell us about the continuing existence of a separate Cornish identity.

Stepping back to 1066 in the first instance, Harold knew as he was crowned that his position was not a safe one. As such he drew up the Fyrd, the reserve army of Anglo-Saxon England, as well as the various thanes and lords from around the realm who would have brought their own professional retainers or warbands with them. The *Chronicle* describes the build-up of forces:

> And king Harold, his brother, gathered so great a ship-force, and also a land-force, as no king here in the land had before done; because it was made known to him that William the bastard would come hither and win this land; all as it afterwards happened.

As we have seen, military service to the crown was by now an established obligation held by the Cornish nobility in exchange for their lands and titles being recognised within the English state. As such it is inconceivable that forces from Cornwall and the wider West Country were not part of this huge gathering, the largest known at the time. Unlike the northern earls, Edwin and Morcar, who seem to have kept their forces in the north and will eventually engage Harald Hardrada in an unsuccessful battle at Fulford Gate, there was no lurking enemy likely to attack Cornwall or Devon. Hardrada, in comparison, was a known threat who Harold would also have been aware of.

While it is true that there could be an argument for keeping the western-most forces in place, in case of an attack elsewhere on the south coast, Harold knew that William was likely to muster his forces in Normandy, close to his own centre of power, rather than in lands controlled by one of his allied vassals such as the Bretons or William of Poitiers. As such, his shortest route to cross the Channel would have put him on the south coast near to Hastings.

Another consideration he no doubt had to contend with were that many of the Godwins' traditional lands were in that region of England. If Harold left them unprotected he would be seen to specifically have failed in the most crucial role of an Early Medieval lord – being the protector of his people. While Harold's elevated station meant this could apply to anywhere in England, to lose his own personal property would be seen as an unacceptable loss of face.

Still, as we have discussed, lordship in Early Medieval Britain was not one-sided and indeed relied on reciprocal duties. As the months wore on and William, who was having problems both marshalling his forces and contending with the weather, failed to appear, Harold was eventually forced to send his gathered forces back home to their farms so that they could attend to the harvest. This is recorded in the 'C' version of the *Chronicle*, although it is curiously absent in other versions:

> When it was the Nativity of St. Mary, then were the men's provisions gone, and no man could any longer keep them there. Then were the men allowed to go home, and the king rode up, and the ships were despatched to London; and many perished before they came thither. When the ships had reached home, then came king Harold from Norway, north into Tyne, and unawares, with a very large ship-force, and no small one; that might be, or more. And Tosty the earl came to him with all that he had gotten, all as they had before agreed; and then they went both, with all the fleet, along the Ouse, up towards York. Then was it made known to king Harold in the south, as he was come from on shipboard, that Harold king of Norway and Tosty the earl were landed near York.

The Nativity of St Mary is 8 September, in other words it effectively marks the end of summer which would be the traditional campaigning season. The army that had been assembled would therefore have met their obligations to Harold and he would have had to release them back to their normal lives. More than this, while the image of a plucky peasant Fyrd has more basis in Victorian fantasy than in reality, the members of the Fyrd would still have been farm owners and landholders, the sorts of people needed to oversee the harvest and ensure proper storage for winter. If Harold held them away from their work for too long, it could risk famine and starvation over the cold months ahead.

Of course, it ended up being terrible timing for Harold, and he was forced to gather what forces he could on the forced march northwards to confront Hardrada. Given the location in the far north-east it is very unlikely that the forces he assembled included any of the western Fyrd or many of the lords from that region. Indeed, as we shall discuss in a moment, it would appear that at least some of these forces remained at a strength that could have helped challenge the various invaders.

What is notable is that the western forces don't seem to have rejoined Harold when he returned from the north to face William at Hastings (given their later presence at Exeter). It is possible that they had dispersed too far into the West Country to make the return trip in time; after all, Harold's journey is famously swift, and there are certainly those historians who now argue he should have pursued a more cautious course and waited for the men he had sent away to rejoin him. It should be noted however that William, upon arriving in England, immediately set about harrying the lands around Hastings where the Normans had constructed a castle.

As previously noted, these were Harold's own ancestral lands that were being burnt and it's impossible that this was anything other than a conscious decision on William's part. He would have heard about Harold's absence very soon after he landed and, further, would have wanted to bring him to battle as soon as possible. By burning and harrying Harold's lands (as depicted in the Bayeux Tapestry), he was directly challenging his authority and, more than that, shaming him as a lord. Harold could not afford to delay his return if he hoped to retain the loyalty of his forces, some of which may already have been suspect.

For example, the western lords, having already been seen to do their duty in the summer, may have lingered intentionally. It was only fifteen years since Harold had despoiled Devon, Somerset and possibly parts of Cornwall, and had killed at least some of the leading men of those regions.

As such, it is possible that they would have been less inclined to rush back to his aid, king or not. After all, the swiftness of the resulting Norman takeover and success against the various uprisings that opposed it are almost as stunning as William's victory at Hastings itself. For a population that was, particularly by the eleventh century, somewhat used to warfare with various invaders where, nevertheless, a certain amount of status quo remained in place, it is not inconceivable that they would have left Harold hanging, particularly given the excuse that their obedience in the summer provided, secure in the belief that even if he fell in battle there would be another Anglo-Saxon king to replace him.

Nor would they have been alone in this hesitancy. Lawson [2002] suggests that Harold may have declined to bring the northern earls, Edwin and Morcar, and their forces with him because he did not have faith in their loyalty. They were another set of powerful nobles the Godwinsons had stepped on during their long ascent towards power. Specifically, they had frequently clashed with Harold's brother Tostig in the years before he was exiled from the family.

Given the western lords' similar reasons to dislike Harold, it is not unreasonable to suggest that their loyalty would be equally in question.

Whatever the reason for their absence, it meant that the western Fyrd and lords missed out on the slaughter at Senlac Ridge, and Marren [2004] estimates the English casualties to be as high as 4,000 dead. This figure could be as high as 50 per cent of the English on the field that day and, while the Fyrd no doubt bore the brunt, this would have included a large portion of the elite of

England's nobility who seem to have formed around the body of Harold and been slain in large numbers.

This left the West Country, including Cornwall, better off than many areas who were suddenly both lordless and missing significant portions of their menfolk. It is perhaps unsurprising then that Gytha, Harold's mother, with her grandchildren, sought shelter in Exeter following the loss at Hastings. Hoskins [2004] suggests that she is the cause, or at least the rallying point, for a rebellion in the city in 1067. As the *Anglo-Saxon Chronicle* records:

> The king this year imposed a heavy tax on the unfortunate people; but, notwithstanding, he let his men plunder all the country which they passed through: after which he marched to Devonshire and besieged Exeter eighteen days. Many of his army were slain there: but he had promised them well and performed ill: the citizens surrendered the city, because the Thanes had betrayed them. This summer the child Edgar, with his mother Agatha, his sisters Margaret and Christina, Merlesweyne and several good men, went to Scotland under the protection of king Malcolm, who received them all ...
>
> This year Harold's mother, Githa, and the wives of many good men with her, went to the Steep Holmes, and there abode some time; and afterwards went from thence over sea to St. Omer's.

The fact that Gytha flees Exeter after the events of the siege does seem to lend some weight to her involvement in it. The *Chronicle* seems to indicate the siege was a fiercely contested one, which we might expect given Exeter's Roman defences, including the ancient city wall that had been reinforced during the time of Alfred and the Viking invasions. It is interesting to note, though, that there is no mention of the defenders other than, we would assume, the people of Exeter themselves and presumably the retinues of the local nobility.

As we have noted, Harold and his father had done little to inspire loyalty in the West Country. It's also notable that, other than William burning his way through Dorset on the way to Exeter (which would likely have deterred all but the most die-hard loyalists), the campaign seems to be entirely focused on the city. This seems to drive home that the rest of the countryside did not join Gytha and her followers.

William's later campaigns, particularly the infamous Harrying of the North, make clear that he was more than happy to forcibly put down any resistance to his rule, so the fact that his revenge, in this case at least, is so focused suggests that this was a very limited uprising, possibly reinforcing Gytha's proposed role in it.

It is also worth considering the way in which the siege ended, when the citizens surrendered 'because the Thanes had betrayed them'. This suggests that even the population of Exeter (and potentially the Fyrd elements from Devon) were not willing to continue fighting for Godwin's line. A siege is, after all, a brutal affair of frequent tedium and deprivation pockmarked by chaos and battle. The fact that the Normans seem unable to break the defences in their assaults suggests that, had the morale of the citizens been higher, they may have been able to stretch out the battle for many more weeks.

Of course, the nature of the betrayal is not immediately clear. It may equally be that Gytha and her immediate supporters, finding less support than they expected from the surrounding countryside, slipped out of the city and left the inhabitants to fend for themselves.

Whatever the truth of the events, it certainly seems that the Cornish, at least, took no part in the rebellion despite its relative proximity (no more than a day or two's march) to their domains. As we have seen, the *Chronicle* identifies the Cornish separately as late as the 1050s, and even earlier in the same passage the Welsh are brought up as the Britons: 'Child Edric and the Britons were unsettled this year, and fought with the men of the castle at Hereford, to whom they did much harm.'

This would seem to rule out any Cornish participants being lumped into the citizens of Exeter. Additionally, William ends his campaign at Exeter as we have noted. There is no mention of a further expedition into Cornwall, as we might expect had it joined in the rebellion.

Another account of the Siege of Exeter comes from the *Historia Ecclesiastica*, a near-contemporary chronicle of events written in the twelfth century. It was written by a Norman monk, Orderic Vitalis, who was actually born in Shropshire to an English mother. Orderic actually borrows heavily from another, even closer, chronicler: William of Poitiers. However, William was an unabashedly biased source when it came to the Duke of Normandy. His *Gesta Guillelmi* was a praise poem, and had a tendency to brush over any rough spots in the Norman conquest.

To see this in action, we can compare two passages, both to do with the year following the Norman Conquest.

In William's version:

Meanwhile Odo, bishop of Bayeux, and William fitz Osbern were administering their prefectures in the kingdom, each praiseworthy in his own, working sometimes together, sometimes separately; if ever necessity demanded it, one gave speedy help to the other. Their wise vigilance was made all the more effective by the friendly willingness with which they genuinely agreed. They loved each other and the king equally; they burned with a common desire to keep the Christian people in peace, and deferred readily to each other's advice. They paid the greatest respect to justice, as the king had admonished, so that fierce men and enemies might be corrected and brought into friendship. The lesser officials were equally zealous in the castles where each had been placed. But neither benefits nor fear could sufficiently force the English to prefer peace and quiet to changes and revolts.

(II, 46)

While Orderic, who was still working in Normandy so shouldn't be entirely considered to be on the English side, describes the same period thus:

the English were groaning under the Norman yoke, and suffering oppressions from the proud lords who ignored the king's injunctions. The petty lords who were guarding the castles oppressed all the native inhabitants of high and low degree, and heaped shameful burdens on them. For Bishop Odo and William fitz Osbern, the king's viceregents, were so swollen with pride that they would not deign to hear the reasonable plea of the English or give them impartial judgement. When their men-at-arms were guilty of plunder and rape they protected them by force, and wreaked their wrath all the more violently upon those who complained of the cruel wrongs they suffered. And so the English groaned aloud for their lost liberty and plotted ceaselessly to find some way of shaking off a yoke that was so intolerable and unaccustomed.

(HE IV: ii, 171–2)

Orderic is supported in this view by the writers of the *Chronicle*, although, as with William, we should expect a certain amount of bias in this regard:

Nevertheless, he laid a tribute on the people, very heavy; and then went, during Lent, over sea to Normandy, and took with him archbishop Stigand, and Aylnoth, abbat of Glastonbury, and child Edgar, and Edwin the earl, and Morkar the earl, and Waltheof the earl, and many other good men of land. And bishop Odo and William the earl remained here behind, and they built castles wide throughout the nation, and poor people distressed; and ever after it greatly grew in evil. May the end be good when God will!

Of the three, Orderic's account seems the most balanced, so it is this that we will rely upon going forward.

Returning to the Siege of Exeter, Orderic's account opens with an interesting passage:

> Every city and district which he (William) had visited in person or occupied with his garrisons obeyed his will. But in the marches of his kingdom, to the west and north, the inhabitants were still barbarous, and had only obeyed the English king in the time of King Edward and his predecessors when it suited their ends. Exeter was the first town to fight for liberty ... It is a wealthy and ancient city built in a plain, strongly fortified ... A great force of citizens held it, young and old seething with anger against every inhabitant of Gaul. Further, they had repeatedly sent for allies from the neighbouring districts, had detained foreign merchants with any aptitude for war, and had built or restored their towers and battlements as they judged necessary. They sent envoys urging other cities to combine with them in similar measures, and prepared to fight with all their strength against the foreign king, with whom they had had no dealings before that time.
>
> (HE IV: ii, 178–9)

The identification of the inhabitants as 'barbarous' is an interesting one, although given the context it here seems largely to indicate the northern and western Saxons, as well as possibly the Cymry in Wales. There is a possibility that the Cornish are included in this measure, and certainly the idea of a loyalty to the English crown only so far as it served them in turn is a fair description of what we have seen prior to the Norman invasion.

Despite this, it seems clear from the actions of the rebels in this passage that they make desperate attempts to rally additional support and, so far as we are told, none seem to be successful. This further supports a general lack of enthusiasm for the rebellion in both Devon and Cornwall, making it much clearer cut than the Saxon sources alone.

However, Orderic added another interesting detail during William's march west: 'he marched on them in force, and for the first time called out Englishmen in his army' (HE IV: ii, 180).

This is a fairly unequivocal endorsement that some former vassals of the English state had relatively quickly adjusted to the new status quo. This is actually a continuation of something he notes in an earlier passage: 'At that time too some of the most able citizens of the towns, some native knights of wealth and good name, and many of the common people rose unequivocally on the Norman side against their fellow countrymen' (HE IV: ii, 176–7).

As we shall soon see, there is good reason to suspect that many of the Cornish elites who retained their rank would have been among this number. The wider acknowledgement of loyal vassals among the former English elite also seems to reinforce the possibility that, western or not, the Cornish were not among the 'barbarous people' Orderic previously identified.

As regards the actual battle, both the *Chronicle* and Orderic seem to be in agreement about the difficulties the attackers faced: 'for many days he fought relentlessly to drive the citizens from the ramparts and undermine the walls. Finally the citizens were compelled by the unremitting attacks of the enemy to take wiser counsel and humbly plead for pardon' (HE IV: ii, 180).

For Orderic, the people turn on the rebellion because they 'take wiser counsel', which could well mean that the people turned on the rebel leaders as we suggested earlier. Orderic is also, of course, at pains to stress how magnanimous in victory William is. As noted, there doesn't seem to be any looting or burning of Exeter, although the construction of Rougemont Castle does follow fairly swiftly after the rebellion. Of course, the lack of reprisal may represent a negotiated end to the siege. William promised to leave the people alone (possibly as the ringleaders had already fled) and in turn they opened the gates and spared him the loss of any more men.

While the people of the south-west may have indicated their desire to be done with Godwin and his line, it would appear that they were not yet done with the south-west. Later in 1067, a large fleet led by the sons of Harold Godwinson sailed from Ireland, where they had taken shelter after 1066, and landed in the Severn Estuary and advanced on Bristol.

There is some confusion about how many of his sons took part in this sudden invasion; however, a number of sources all agree that it took place. It would seem, based on their initial actions at least, that the brothers had hoped to meet friendly support when they landed in much the same way that the rebellion in Exeter had desperately lobbied for support from the surrounding countryside. However, when they reached Bristol, the town shut its gates to them and resisted their attempts at entry. As the *Chronicle* puts it:

During these things one of Harold's sons [the singular has been identified as a copyist error by Plummer, 1899] came with a fleet from Ireland unexpectedly into the mouth of the river Avon, and soon plundered all that neighbourhood. They went to Bristol, and would have stormed the town, but the inhabitants opposed them bravely. Seeing they could get nothing from the town, they went to their ships with the booty they had got by plundering, and went to Somersetshire, where they went up the country. Ednoth, master of the horse, fought with them, but he was slain there, and many good men on both sides; and those who were left departed thence.

Again, plunder seems to be the order of the day once a successful rebellion is unlikely to emerge. The lord who eventually opposed them, whose title would more closely be translated as 'Eadnoth the Staller', is himself a holdo-ver from the pre-Norman aristocracy, having held his position as Staller, or Horse Master, for King Edward, as made clear by a charter from Edward to Ednoth [S1129]. This confrontation, although fatal for Ednoth, drives home just how isolated Harold's family truly were in the new order. Far from being the native favourites struggling against a new and foreign oppressor, they seem to become something of a nuisance, particularly in the south-west.

According to a separate chronicle, that of Florence of Worcester, the sons: 'having gained the victory, and carried away a considerable spoil from Devon and Cornwall, returned to Ireland'.

Further raiding in Devon and Cornwall isn't recorded elsewhere. However, the Exon book records, in a note scribbled into a margin on Folio 323r, that: 'These 9 estates just mentioned have been ruined by men from Ireland.'

All nine estates are in south Devon, suggesting that the brothers may have raided their way around Land's End in the manner of their father before them. If the nine burnt estates are linked to Harold's sons, then it would have been yet another mark against them in the local psyche and so perhaps it is no surprise that when the brothers chose to raid the south-west again, landing in north Devon this time, there was not only a lack of local support but they were actually met and defeated by Brian of Brittany, the local earl, and forces drawn from the surrounding countryside:

> After this came Harold's sons from Ireland, about Midsummer, with sixty-four ships and entered the mouth of the Taff [the Taw], where they incautiously landed. Earl Brian came upon them unawares with a large army, and slew all their bravest men: the others escaped to their ships, and Harold's sons went back again to Ireland.

A fuller account of the battle is given by William of Jumieres in his *Gesta Normannorum Ducum*, or 'The Deeds of the Norman Dukes', written, again, nearly contemporary to events:

> Meanwhile two sons of King Harold had separated themselves from the company of these rebels and accompanied by their father's household troops

went to the king of the Irish, called Dermot, to ask his support. After a short but favourable stay in Ireland, where they gathered a large army, they returned to England with sixty-six ships to a site which they considered most strategic, for an attack, where, like most dangerous pirates, they laid waste by robbery and fire to the country's population. Forthwith Brian, son of Odo, count of the Bretons, came up against them and in the course of two battles fought in one day he defeated them.

One thousand and seven hundred warriors, some of whom were magnates of the realm, perished, others fled from the battlefield and somehow escaped death by fleeing with their ships. With deep mourning they reported the loss of their dear brothers to the Irish. It is even said that if night had not put an end to the battle, all would have been cut down by death's razor.

The battle site for this clash has been identified relatively recently by Nick Arnold as Northam, a small North Devon town near Appledore. While estimating the size of Early Medieval battles can be extremely difficult, we can imagine the battle must have been a significant clash.

One of the ships at the Viking Ship Museum in Roskilde, *Skuldelev 2*, is identified as a warship crafted in the 1040s in Dublin [Skipmuseet]; as such, it seems a reasonable building block for estimating the brothers' fleet. The *Skuldelev 2* could hold somewhere between sixty-five and seventy men, the majority of whom would also be warriors. This means that, if all the ships were fully crewed and of a similar size, the brothers may have led a force of over 4,000 men.

To oppose this effectively Brian must have led a force of similar size, which must have required relying on local forces from Devon, Cornwall and Somerset. This is doubly the case as, during this same year, William was busy subduing a revolt in the north alongside a large force of his Norman knights. Therefore there could have been little hope of reinforcement from that quarter. As the earlier raid showed, the local forces of the south-west would not hesitate to fight on the Norman side of this conflict, so assuming their active support seems safe.

The swiftness of Brian's advance, alongside the potential detail of there being two separate battles in a single day – which would suggest that the brothers' forces may have broken and withdrawn, then been reengaged on the way to their ships – also suggests that Brian's force made significant use of cavalry. For the Breton/Norman forces this would perhaps be expected, but it would also fit the previously described style of warfare practised by the Cornish.

While we can't be sure if a predilection for mounted warfare had survived the centuries since active conflict with Wessex, it seems likely that, mounted or not, the Cornish would have been able to integrate closely with Brian and his Breton vassals, as we'll see shortly. However, there was a final uprising in the south-west during these momentous early years of Norman occupation.

In 1069, a year after Harold's sons had been driven off for the final time, King Swein of Denmark sent a fleet to attack England, apparently at the urging of the English thanes who preferred their former enemies and one time over-lords, the Danes, to their new rulers from Normandy. The arrival of the Danish fleet caused an outbreak of unrest across the country as rebellions old and new resumed with some force, including in the West Country. As Orderic has it:

> The same thing was done at Exeter by the people of Devonshire, and a host of men assembled from Cornwall. It is the extreme point of the west of England towards Ireland, from whence it derives its name of Cornu Britannica, the Horn of Britain, or Cornwall. The citizens of Exeter took the king's side, for they had not forgotten the sufferings they had formerly endured. The king receiving this intelligence lost no time in giving orders to two earls, William and Brian, to march to the relief of the two places which were attacked. But before they reached Shrewsbury, the enemy had burnt the town and retired. The garrison of Exeter made a sudden sally, and charg- ing the besieger with impetuosity, put them to the rout. William and Brian, meeting the fugitives, punished their rash enterprise with a great slaughter.
> (HE IV: v)

This third western uprising isn't mentioned in the *Chronicle*, although the arrival of Swein's fleet and the larger uprising, led by the Atheling Edgar, is covered in some detail. It's also notable that the two locations mentioned here, Shrewsbury and Exeter, are vast distances apart. It does somewhat raise questions as to why Brian and his forces would be sent all the way north to Shrewsbury if there was a simultaneous uprising in Devon and Cornwall.

Given the sequence of events as described, we can perhaps assume that the Shrewsbury uprising happened first, the latest front in Eadric the Wild's ongoing resistance to Norman rule. William, who would have seen the lack of enthusiasm we have discussed in the West Country for the Godwinson rebellions, may have felt it safe to send Brian and his forces north to assist on that front.

However, with word of the Danish fleet's arrival and the uprising around York no doubt spreading rapidly, and the bulk of Norman forces in the region moving northwards, it would perhaps seem an ideal time for disaffected thanes, and Cornish lords, to attempt to seize the country.

The specific and highly detailed mention of Cornwall in this instance can leave little doubt that at least some of the Cornish elite took part in this rising, while also reaffirming their apathy towards the previous revolts. It is also difficult to see a reason for this change of heart other than a personal dislike or vendetta against Harold and his heirs.

Personal loyalty and feuds are right at the heart of Early Medieval politics, and the uprising in 1069 seems to seal the case for a resentment towards Harold and his heirs in the West Country which perhaps undermined their own attempts at regaining power.

As for the change of heart, it is possible that many in the West Country retained loyalty towards Cnut and his heirs. Even if the oft-repeated story of Cnut granting Cornwall its independence is not true, we can certainly see a significant number of Anglo-Danish finds in the archaeological record from around the time of his rule (for example CORN-FB5995, a stirrup with an early depiction of a lion upon it). We have also seen the evidence for a not insignificant amount of Hiberno-Norse settlement in Cornwall and it's possible these groups would look favourably on a renewed Scandinavian kingship. Therefore, there could have been a number of lords or landowners willing to rebel in support of the Danes, but who were apathetic, or even openly hostile, to the efforts of Harold's family.

Of course, from Orderic's description at least, it would appear that it was the rebels' turn to feel the consequences of past actions as the citizens of Exeter, perhaps motivated more by the pleas for assistance that had been ignored by their neighbours than by any loyalty to William or his past generosity, used the same defences that had frustrated William to stop the forces attacking them.

The fact that the garrison was eventually able to sally to drive over the besiegers does, however, call into question how many rebels there actually were. Norman garrisons were, in general terms, relatively small, which is one of the reasons they relied upon castle building to such a large degree. With a castle in place, even a relatively small detachment could hold off a much larger force until help eventually arrived or, as was the case at Shrewsbury, didn't arrive.

Given that the garrison, according to Orderic, acts alone and drives out the invaders, it seems likely that it was a relatively small force of rebels, and certainly not the entire strength of Devon and Cornwall. Even if the citizens of Exeter supported the garrison in their sally, it would be expected that a larger force would have been able to overwhelm them in relatively short order.

It's also notable that, following this rebellion, there again does not seem to be any severe backlash in the West Country. There is no western equivalent of the Harrying of the North, for example, despite it, at this point, having had a history of repeated trouble.

Probably the mixed nature of the rebellions, and the fact that so few had seen any widespread support, would have stayed William and Brian's hand. Smaller-scale retribution would be much harder to see; for example, the loss of estates from rebellious lords would probably go somewhat unremarked by the historical record when compared to the slaughter occurring in the north.

This would seem to suggest, despite at least some Cornish involvement in the final rebellion, that it remained a relatively small-scale action. This does, then, bring us back to the question of why the people of the south-west generally, and Cornwall in particular, seemed to be reluctant to rebel against their new overlords despite having ample opportunity in the years following 1066.

At least some of that hesitance is likely the result of who was now in power in the West Country, and the historic links they shared with Cornwall.

12

CORNWALL AND THE BRETONS

Brittany had, in the centuries since its settlement by the Dumnonian elite in the years following the Roman withdrawal, a long history of changing allegiances and levels of sovereignty. Following the liberation of the realm by Alain, Athelstan's foster son, it became a duchy with nominal allegiance to the wider French kingdom in much the same way as Normandy, its close neighbour.

Throughout that time there were ongoing contacts not just with Cornwall, but with all the nations around the Irish Sea and West Atlantic. This is perhaps best evidenced by the continuing development of the Insular style of artwork which can be seen in examples throughout the region, all of which share at least some similarities to one another.

Specific links between Cornwall and Brittany are demonstrated by the *Bodmin Manumissions*, produced in a Breton monastery and delivered to a Cornish one, as well as in the tradition of shared saints which churches in both nations celebrate.

There is also the rather spectacular echo of St Michael's Mount and Mont San Michel in Normandy. While the island of Mont San Michel itself is placed in Normandy, it is only a hair's breadth from the border with Brittany and the lands in this region changed hands many times in the centuries preceding the Norman invasion of England. As such, the community of monks itself no doubt held many Bretons in its ranks. Perhaps this motivated them to petition Edward the Confessor for land in Cornwall, which he granted in a charter of 1037 (S1061), giving them the tidal island of St Michael's Mount as well as another site in Cornwall. It should be noted that the charter of Edward has been called into question, although some historians continue to assert its validity; regardless, it is certainly the case that the two religious communities were linked, with the Cornish Mount acting as a priory of the Norman institution.

Another example of potential cross-Channel landholding comes from Judhael of Totnes, the Breton lord who held vast estates in both Devon and Cornwall at the time of Domesday. It has been suggested that his father, Alfred, is the same Alfred who precedes him in the Domesday Book for Devon in the holding of two manors [17.15-6, fol. 108d]. Judhael, given his importance, is one of the most visible of the new Breton landholders, so it is more than possible that other, less important lords may have had familial links with lands and manors in both Brittany and Cornwall or Devon. If anything this seems extremely likely, given the historic trading and cultural links between north-west France, especially Brittany, and the south-west of Britain.

Returning to the events of 1066 and beyond, William, following a conflict with Duke Conan of Brittany, managed to pull them into his own sphere of influence and many Bretons thus accompanied the invasion force.

When the time came to distribute lands and fiefs in the wake of the Norman victory, many of his Breton subjects took lands further north and east, often around regional centres, usually radiating out from a single powerful lord like William Warrenne. However, a great many others, including Count Brian himself, settled in Devon and Cornwall.

The divide between the Bretons is interesting in itself, with many of the settlers in the south-west coming from the eastern and southern regions of Brittany; while those who settled elsewhere appear to largely hail from north-ern and western Brittany [Keats-Rohan, 1992]. It has been suggested that this reflects a political divide in Brittany between the Marcher lords of the Breton–Norman border and those from deeper within Brittany.

Certainly there seems to be some support for this viewpoint. The lords from around Dol, in particular, don't appear to have supported Duke Conan in his conflict with William immediately prior to the Norman invasion and may have tacitly supported William instead. Aspects of this conflict will eventually rear their head again in the chaos of the Anarchy centuries later, but for now it perhaps gave William a good reason to keep his retainers spread apart from one another.

It is interesting to note that a majority of the landholders in Devon and Cornwall, at least by the time of Domesday, appear to be either Bretons or Norman lords from the Breton Marches. These are Normans who held lands in the Cotentin Peninsula and similar regions; areas that had, as recently as the tenth century, been in Breton hands and who most likely had at least some familiarity with Breton language and customs. Given the apparent cooperation between the two groups, it is also likely that the Norman lords would have had at least some Breton followers of their own.

Their settlement in the south-west can, if their assumed early support of William is believed, be seen as a reward for service. After all, ignoring the long-standing links between the two regions, Cornwall and Brittany are geographically extremely close together and were both linked into the long-standing trade networks of the Irish Sea and Western Atlantic, as we have seen. This would have made administering their new holdings while staying in touch with the homeland much simpler than it was for those whose awarded lands were much further up country.

In reality, the desirability of Cornwall in particular for Breton lords and their Marcher associates should be obvious. Rather than attempting to impose an entirely new language and culture onto a resentful populace, as many Norman lords faced in their English holdings, the rulers of Cornwall now spoke, if not the same language, then certainly a language that was still mutually intelligible. Indeed, even in the modern age Cornish and Breton remain much more closely related than either does to Welsh, despite all coming from the same shared Brythonic ancestor. The famous letter of William Bodinar even relates of a Cornish fisherman being able to make himself understood to Bretons as late as the eighteenth century.

This shared culture and language must have done a considerable amount to smooth out the transitional period. If we compare the Norman/Breton invasion to the long conflict with Wessex, it seems clear that the 'invaders' in the former case would have been significantly less disruptive culturally then the latter were. Of course, that does not mean the transition was a smooth one.

As we have noted previously, the Cornish were active participants in the Irish Sea slave trade and this trade would come to an end under William's watch. While Cornwall maintained a high slave population during the time of the Domesday Book in 1086, the active trade of slaves to Ireland and beyond had been banned by William around 1070.

William of Malmesbury records it thus:

At his instigation also was abolished the infamous custom of those ill-disposed people who used to sell their slaves into Ireland. The credit of this action, I know not exactly whether to attribute to Lanfranc [the new Archbishop of Canterbury and William's personal moral tutor], or to Wulstan bishop of Worcester; who would scarcely have induced the king, reluctant from the profit it produced him, to this measure, had not Lanfranc commended it.

While we have covered the occasional exaggeration in William's chronicles previously, it does seem that the Conqueror was moved to ban the slave trade as his own laws record: 'I prohibit the sale of any man by another outside the country on pain of a fine to be paid in full to me.'

This made the king's feelings on the subject very clear, and would have been hugely disruptive to the Cornish economy (as well as that of Bristol, further along the coast). The timing of the laws (around 1070) also may provide some perspective on why there was Cornish support for the final stage of rebellions. It may well be that those lords or landholders who relied most heavily on the slave trade to provide their wealth turned against William and the Bretons at this stage.

Additionally, society itself was being rapidly overhauled under the new feudal system that the invaders brought with them from the Continent. This meant that, while slavery may well have been abolished, the lot of poor freemen was suddenly much reduced as they became tied inextricably to specific areas of land and lords.

Still, the changes seem to be at least somewhat cushioned in Cornwall by the arrival of the Breton lords and their patronage of local institutions. As Insley [2013] points out, many churches that had negotiated geld-free status with the English state maintain this status after 1066. There also appears to be some continuity in leading figures of these institutions, although they are eventually replaced by Norman incomers.

It may be, considering the example of Mont St Michel and the *Bodmin Gospels*, that there was always some level of cooperation or mutual acknowledgement between the religious institutions in both regions and this came to the Cornish Church's aid after the invasion.

Equally it may be that the Cornish priests enjoyed better relations with the Breton lords above them because of all they shared in common, as discussed earlier. It is probably significant that the *Vocabularium Cornicum* was produced in the century following the conquest, potentially as early as 1150 and certainly in Cornwall by a Cornishman [Jefferson, 2013]. This document is one of the earliest significant records of the Cornish language we have, and the fact of its production suggests that there remains a highly educated Cornish-speaking elite in Cornwall at this date.

It is unlikely that such a work wouldhave been produced if not for the continuing patronage of Cornish institutions that Insley identified. It also laid the groundwork for the renaissance of Cornish literary works which would eventually follow in the thirteenth and fourteenth centuries, with great works like the *Ordinalia* being completed at this time.

It is worth mentioning that there may in fact be a significant corpus of written Cornish works which have been lost to time. We know that Glasney College at one time held a significant library of manuscripts but it was destroyed, along with most of the works it held, during the dissolution of the monasteries, and we will never be sure of the full extent of the loss.

The arrival of the Bretons can therefore be seen to influence a strengthening of the separate Cornish identity, which had continued throughout the Anglo-Saxon period following the end of hostilities in 836.

13

THE END OF THE CONQUEST PERIOD

It is sometimes argued that the influence of Breton lords in Cornwall is over-stated, particularly as Brian of Brittany quits his estates sometime around 1075 and the earls revolt. However, as we have seen, even those lords in the south-west of Norman origin tended to be from the Breton Marches and they, or more likely their followers, are therefore more likely to carry several of the cultural traits we've discussed.

It is also noteworthy that Brian's successor as earl, Robert of Mortain, the king's half-brother, himself had several undertenants and sworn men who were Breton, including Judhael of Totnes who we have already mentioned.

In fact, when we look at the list of chief tenants for Cornwall in the Domesday Book there is only a single figure who is neither linked to Brittany or to a local religious institution [Thorn, 1979]. The only outlier, a man named Gotshelm, is also the smallest landowner, so can perhaps be safely regarded as something of an outlier.

One important change that Robert of Mortain did bring with him as earl is the construction of Launceston Castle. This effectively made Launceston the capital of the Cornish earldom and the town would eventually overtake Bodmin as the largest urban area in Cornwall.

As we have discussed previously, Launceston was the best connected town with the rest of England as the Tamar proved a formidable barrier for foot traffic heading towards southern Cornwall. Thus its use as the capital makes sense. Additional castles were built around Cornwall, but none of them seemed to see any particular action in the years that followed (at least from native Cornish forces) and their eventual loss of usage is quite reminiscent of the

Roman marching forts that preceded them. They are there for a function, but one that is very rarely tested.

For the Cornish it appears this was another situation to be adapted to. It is perhaps fitting, then, that the Anglo-Norman period in Cornwall would eventually come to an end with the founding of one of the most powerful symbols of a separate Cornish identity: the Cornish Stannary.

As we have described throughout this book, tin mining has always been central to the Cornish economy and that remained true no matter who was nominally in control of the territory. The Cornish tin miners, who had preserved their identity in the face of the Romans, Saxons and then the Normans, managed to leverage their specialised skills and the still increasing demand for tin into a series of significant concessions from King John in 1201:

The King to the Archbishops, etc., greeting ... John, by the grace of God, King of England, etc., to the archbishops, bishops, abbots, earls, barons, judges, sheriffs, foresters, and to all our bailiffs and faithful people, greeting. Be it known that we have granted that all tin miners of Cornwall and Devon are free of pleas of the natives as long as they work for the profit of our ferm or for the marks for our new tax; for the stannaries are on our demesne. And they may dig for tin, and for turf for smelting it, at all times freely and peaceably without hindrance from any man, on the moors and in the fiefs of bishops, abbots, and earls, as they have been accustomed to do. And they may buy faggots to smelt the tin, without waste of forest, and they may divert streams for their work just as they have been accustomed to do by ancient usage. Nor shall they desist from their work by reason of any summons, except those of the chief warden of the stannaries or his bailiffs.

We have granted also that the chief warden of the stannaries and his bailiffs have plenary power over the miners to do justice to them and to hold them to the law. And if it should happen that any of the miners ought to be seized and imprisoned for breach of the law they should be received in our prisons; and if any of them should become a fugitive or outlaw let his chattels be delivered to us by the hands of the warden of the stannaries because the miners are of our ferm and always in our demesne. Moreover, we have granted to the treasurer and the weighers, so that they might be more faithful and attentive to our service in guarding our treasure in market towns, that they shall be quit in all towns in which they stay of aids and tallages as long as they are in our service as treasurers and weighers; for they have and can have nothing else throughout the year for their services to us.

The king's charter, acknowledging the 'ancient usage' rights of the tin miners, can, in some ways, be seen as a reminder of the separate status that the Cornish had struggled to secure for themselves throughout the centuries. It represents a major disruption of the feudal social order in order to accommodate the rights and desires of tin miners. The land, the forests and streams of Cornwall remained exclusively for their use and it was only their own people who could regulate them.

Interestingly, it is also the birth of the stannaries that perhaps gives us one of the longest lasting, and most well-known, elements of the modern Cornish identity: St Piran.

Before the Stannary period, St Piran was just one of a number of Cornish saints, some of whom we have touched on in our earlier discussion. However, sometime in the fourteenth century, when the Devonshire Stannary was being negotiated, a monk at Tavistock Abbey completed a vita of the saint's life that included the now famous story of Piran and his altar.

The short version of this tale is that Piran, praying one day at his stone altar, was amazed as the altar cracked and bubbling white metal formed a cross atop of it. This image of the white cross on black then became the inspiration for the Cornish flag itself, although the actual dating of the flag is difficult to ascertain (it is perhaps worth noting that the Breton flag, the Kroz Du, which is the inverse of Piran's Cross, starts to appear around this same time period).

Thus did Piran rediscover tin mining, the implication of the story being that the knowledge had been lost some time after the Romans left. Of course, we have demonstrated there is no way this story is accurate, as there was no end of mining between the Romans leaving and the time the vita was written. It is also worth pointing out that the majority of the vita, in the form in which it survives, is actually taken from the life of an Irish Saint, St Ciaran.

So the tale of St Piran seems somewhat suspect when looked at in this light, at least this most famous part of it, and at least as a record of historical events. However, as a tale used to add ecclesiastical approval to the newly formed institutions of the stannaries, it perhaps makes much more sense.

As such, the cross of Piran, and the tale, remain an excellent symbol for the Cornish. It is a story that adapted itself to suit the needs of the people whoneeded it, just as the Cornish elites adapted to preserve their unique identity in the face of waves of invasion and strife.

CONCLUSION

Following the Early Medieval period and Anglo-Norman period the existential threat to the Cornish identity, which the invasions of Wessex once represented, was no more. The Cornish were recognised as a separate entity within England. Not their own country, perhaps, but also not wholly in line with the crown.

The rebellions in 1497 and 1549 would damage this identity, both through the deaths of native Cornish speakers and due to an increased hostility from the English state towards Cornish matters. The failure of a Cornish-language version of the Bible to be printed, for example, is often cited as one of the key factors in the decline of the language.

However, while pleasant stories about Molly Pentreath and the 'last speakers' of Cornish make for excellent tales, the reality seems much different. The Cornish language lasts into the eighteenth century and, by the time it is starting to fade out of use, there is a revivalist antiquarian movement ready to record it and preserve its usage into the modern day.

Away from language, the culture of Cornwall continued to be noticeably different from that of England, even into the present day. Traditional sports like wrestling and hurling still have modern adherents, while the bardic movement of the nineteenth century would one day herald the Gorsedd Kernow, or Bards of Cornwall, who are enthusiastic advocates and shepherds of Cornwall's cultural heritage.

Overall, the twenty-first century seems to be a time of revival for all things Cornish, as local people once more take pride and comfort in a heritage that, for a short time at least, seemed to be disappearing.

It is unlikely any of this could have been the case were it not for the actions of the Cornish, noble and commoner, during the vital years of the Early Medieval period. From preserving their trade routes, and thus their stability, during the chaotic years following Roman withdrawal, through to achieving military victories like the key Battle of Hehil, the ancestors of the Cornish took decisive action in the time between the fifth and eleventh centuries to ensure that their descendants would have a culture, a language and a land that they still recognised.

Crucially, of course, they also knew when to stop fighting and adapt. When the wars of the eighth and ninth centuries raged towards their end and it became clear that military defeat of Wessex would not be possible, they negotiated a peace that saw local power secured, albeit underneath the throne of the Saxon.

As the Great Heathen Army invaded they took care to make peace with both Vikings and Saxons, perhaps biding their time to see which way the conflict eventually would turn. We will never know for sure if there were voices urging a new attack on Wessex, but history would prove cooler heads correct. It is unlikely the eventual peace and integration that Athelstan secured in the tenth century would have ever been achieved had Cornwall attacked the English in earnest.

The peace that Athelstan worked with the Cornish, and the border now officially set with the Tamar, would last into the modern day. Where aggression and conquest had failed, fairly simple acts of concession and compromise brought Cornwall into the English fold.

Throughout all of this, the mining of tin provided not only economic boons, but also an invaluable and highly specialised skill that would become inseparably linked with Cornish identity and, one day, would be hugely significant around the world. This was recognised by UNESCO in its designation of Cornish mining as a World Heritage Site.

When the Anglo-Saxon period ended, despite the best efforts of the marauding Godwinsons, the Norman invasion saw a cultural revival in Cornwall led by its own distant relations, the Bretons, which would one day see great works of Cornish literature produced, although many others may well have been lost in the destruction of Glasney College.

Finally, these latter two facets would combine to form the Stannary and its attendant parliament, perhaps the strongest symbol of Cornish self-determination since the time of the kingdom of Kernow itself.

So it is that, if we look for the foundation of Kernow, of the Western Kingdom, we have to look at the Early Medieval period and the tangled network of events, alliances and battles that brought the country into being.

The survival of the Cornish identity does not, of course, mean it is now without threats. There are still many issues facing young Cornish people, and other natives of the south-west, largely linked to economic difficulties and the problems of second home ownership and unsustainable cost of living increases. These problems deserve urgent attention and improvement; the irony of economic realities succeeding where conquest and invasion failed would be extremely bitter to swallow.

However, it is also important to understand the history, the shared heritage, which helps to make the south-west in general, and Cornwall in particular, such a special and unique place.

In some small way, I hope this work adds to that.

BIBLIOGRAPHY

Books

Charles-Edwards, T., *Wales and the Britons 350–1064* (Oxford: Oxford University Press, 2015)

Cole, A., *The Place-Name Evidence for a Routeway Network in Anglo Saxon England* (thesis) (Kellogg College, Oxford, 2010)

Cunliffe, Barry, *Iron Age Communities in Britain: An Account of England, Scotland and Wales from the Seventh Century BC Until the Roman Conquest*, 4th ed. (Routledge, 2005). pp201–06

Dark, K.R., *Civitas to kingdom: British Political Continuity 300–800* (London: Leicester University Press, 1994)

Davies, S., *War and Society in Medieval Wales 633–1283,* 1st ed. (Cardiff: University of Wales Press, 2014)

Davies, W., 'The Latin Charter-Tradition in Western Britain, Brittany and Ireland in the Early Medieval Period', in *Ireland in Early Medieval Europe: Studies in Memory of Kathleen Hughes*, ed. D. Whitelock, R. McKitterick and D. Dumville (Cambridge, 1982)

Deacon, Bernard, *Cornwall's First Golden Age: From Arthur to the Normans* (London: Francis Boutle Publishers, 2016)

Dodd, L *Official Power and Local Elites in the Roman Provinces*, 188-208 (Routledge, 2016)

Durandus, William, *The Symbolism of Churches and Church Ornaments, with an Introductory Essay by John Mason Neale and Benjamin Webb*, 3rd ed. (London: Gibbings, 1906)

Ellis, Peter Berresford, *Celt and Saxon: The Struggle for Britain AD 410–937* (London: Constable & Co., 1994)

Frere, Sheppard Sunderland, *Britannia: A History of Roman Britain*, 3rd revised ed. (London: Routledge & Kegan Paul, 1987)

Gelling, Margaret, *Place Names in the Landscape* (London: Weidenfeld & Nicolson, 1993)

Gravett, Christopher, *Hastings 1066: The Fall of Saxon England*, Campaign, Vol. 13 (Oxford, UK: Osprey, 1992)

Grinsell, Leslie, *The Archaeology of Wessex* (London: Methuen, 1958)

Guilelmus and Davis, R., *The Gesta Gvillelmi of William of Poitiers* (Oxford: Clarendon Press, 2006)

Hadley, D.M. and Richards, J.D., *The Viking Great Army and the Making of England* (London: Thames & Hudson, 2021)

Halsall, Guy, *Worlds of Arthur: Facts & Fictions of the Dark Ages* (Oxford: Oxford University Press, 2013)

Henley, G. and Byron Smith, J., *A Companion to Geoffrey of Monmouth* (Leiden: Brill, 2020)

Higham, Robert, *Making Anglo-Saxon Devon* (Exeter: The Mint Press, 2008)

Hoskins, W.G., *Two Thousand Years in Exeter* (Revised and updated ed.) (Chichester: Phillimore, 2004) pp. 25–26

Hoskins, W. and Finberg, H., *The Westward Expansion of Wessex* (Leicester: Leicester University Press, 1970)

Jefferson, Judith, *Multilingualism in Medieval Britain (c.1066–1520): Sources and Analysis* (Turnhout: Brepols, 2013) p.59

Kirby, D.P., *The Earliest English Kings* (London: Routledge, 1992)

Lawson, M.K., *The Battle of Hastings: 1066* (Stroud, UK: Tempus, 2002)

Lewis, G.R., *The Stannaries* (Boston: Houghton Mifflin, 1908)

Marren, P., *1066: The Battles of York, Stamford Bridge and Hastings* (Havertown: Pen & Sword, 2004)

Morris, J., *The Age of Arthur* (Londn: Phoenix, 1995) p.307

Myres, J. (1986). The English settlements. Oxford: Clarendon.

Olson, L., *Early monasteries in Cornwall* (Woodbridge, Suffolk: Boydell Press, 1989) pp.62–65.

Orderic and Chibnall, M., *The Ecclesiastical History of Orderic Vitalis* (Oxford: Clarendon Press, 1980)

Padel, O.J., 'The Charter of Lanlawren (Cornwall)', *Latin Learning and English Lore (Volumes I & II): Studies in Anglo-Saxon Literature for Michael Lapidge*, ed. Katherine O'Brien O'Keeffe and Andy Orchard (Toronto: University of Toronto Press, 2016) pp. 74–85

Pelteret, D., *Slavery in Early Mediaeval England from the Reign of Alfred until the Twelfth Century* (Studies in Anglo-Saxon History, 7) (Woodbridge: Boydell, 2001) pp.229–31

Plummer, Charles, *Two of the Saxon Chronicles Parallel, Vol. 2* (1899)

Pool, P.A.S., *William Bodinar's Letter, 1776* (Journal of the Royal Institution of Cornwall, 1975)

Probert, D., *Church and Landscape: A Study in Social Transition in South West Britain AD 400 to 1200* (PhD) (University of Birmingham, 2002)

Simeon and Stevenson, J., *The Historical Works of Simeon of Durham* (London: Seeleys, 1885)

Skene, W.F., Bryce, Derek (ed.), *Arthur and the Britons in Wales and Scotland*, illustrated ed., edited by Derek Bryce. (Lampeter, Wales: Llanerch Press, 1988)

Smart, C., *A Roman Military Complex and Medieval Settlement on Church Hill, Calstock, Cornwall* (Oxford: British Archaeological Reports, 2014)

Thompson, E.A., *St Germanus of Auxerre and the End of Roman Britain* (Woodbridge: Boydell Press, 1984)

Thorn, Caroline and Frank (eds.), *Domesday Book* (Morris, John, gen. ed.) Vol. 10, Cornwall (Chichester: Phillimore, 1979)

Thorpe, B. (1861). The Anglo-Saxon Chronicle, According to the Several Original Authorities. 2nd ed. London: Longman, Green, Longman and Roberts

Todd, Malcolm, *The South West to AD 1000* (London: Longman, 1987), pp. 272–73

Underwood, Richard, *Anglo-Saxon Weapons and Warfare* (Stroud: Tempus, 1999)

Vance, Norman, *The Victorians and Ancient Rome* (Oxford: Blackwell, 1997)

van Houts, Elisabeth M.C. (ed.), *The 'Gesta Normannorum ducum' of William of Jumièges, Orderic Vitalis, and Robert of Torigni*, 1: Introduction and Books I–IV; 2: Books V–VIII. 1995) Oxford: Oxford University Press.

Wasyliw, Patricia Healy, *Martyrdom, Murder, and Magic: Child Saints and Their Cults in Medieval Europe* (Oxford: Peter Lang, 2008)

Worcester, W. and Harvey, J., *Itineraries [of] William Worcestre* (Oxford: Clarendon Press, 1969) p.21

Yorke, Barbara, *Kings and Kingdoms of Early Anglo-Saxon England* (London: Seaby, 1990)

Zosimus, *The History of Count Zosimus: Sometime Advocate and Chancellor of the Roman Empire* (London: J. Davis, 1814)

Articles

Agate, A., Duggan, M., Roskams, S., Turner, S., Campbell, E., Hall, A., Kinnaird, T., Luke, Y., McIntosh, F., Neal, C. and Young, R., 'Early Medieval Settlement at Mothecombe, Devon: The Interaction of Local, Regional and Long-Distance Dynamics', *Archaeological Journal*, 169:1, 2012, pp.343–94.

Barrett, Anthony A., 'Saint Germanus and the British Missions', *Britannia*, vol. 40 [Society for the Promotion of Roman Studies, Cambridge University Press], 2009, pp.197–218, www.jstor.org/stable/27793240.

Biek, L., 'Tin ingots found at Praa Sands, Breage, in 1974', *Cornish Archaeology*, 33, 1994, pp.57–70.

Biggam, C.P., 'Knowledge of Whelk Dyes and Pigments in Anglo-Saxon England', *Anglo-Saxon England*, vol. 35, Cambridge University Press, 2006, pp.23–55.

Finberg, H.P.R., 'Sherborne, Glastonbury, and the Expansion of Wessex', *Transactions of the Royal Historical Society*, vol. 3, Cambridge University Press, 1953, pp.101–24, doi. org/10.2307/3678711.

Halloran, Kevin, 'Welsh Kings at the English Court, 928–956', *The Welsh History Review / Cylchgrawn Hanes Cymru*, 25:3, 2011, pp.297–313. Web.

Hamerow, H., C. Ferguson and J. Naylor, 'The Origins of Wessex Pilot Project', *Oxoniensia*, 78, 2013: pp.49–69.

Higham, Nick, 'Edward the Elder's Reputation: An Introduction', in N.J. Higham and D.H. Hill (eds.), *Edward the Elder, 899–924* (Abingdon, UK: Routledge, 2001), pp. 1–11.

Hill, D., 'The Burghal Hidage: The Establishment of a Text', *Medieval Archaeology*, 13(1), 1969, pp.84–92.

Insley, C., 'Kings and Lords in Tenth-Century Cornwall', *History*, 98(329), 2013, pp.2–22.

Keats-Rohan, K., 'The Bretons and Normans of England 1066–1154: the Family, the Fief and the Feudal Monarchy', *Nottingham Medieval Studies*, 36, 1992, pp.42–78.

Leslie, S., Winney, B., Hellenthal, G. et al., 'The fine-scale genetic structure of the British population', *Nature*, 519, 2015, pp.309–14. doi.org/10.1038/nature14230

Meharg, A.A., Edwards, K.J., Schofield, J.E., Raab, A., Feldmann, J., Moran, A., Bryant, C.L., Thornton, B. and Dawson, J.J.C. 'First comprehensive peat depositional records for tin, lead and copper associated with the antiquity of Europe's largest cassiterite deposits', *Journal of Archaeological Science*, Vol. 39, Issue 3, 2012, pp. 717–27.

Picken, W.M., 'Bishop Wulfsige: An Unrecognised Tenth-Century Gloss in the Bodmin Gospels', *Journal of Cornish Studies*, xiv, 1986, pp.34–8.

Preston-Jones, A., & Rose, P. (1986). 'Medieval Cornwall', *Journal of Cornish Archaeology*, 140.

Reed, S., Bidwell, P. and Allan, J., 'Excavation at Bantham, South Devon, and Post-Roman Trade in South-West England', *Medieval Archaeology*, 55:1, 2011, pp.82–138.

Russell, M., Cheetham, P., Evans, D., Gerdau-Radonic, K., Hambleton, E., Hewitt, I., Manley, H., Speith, N. and Smith, M., 2015. 'The Durotriges Project, Phase Two: An Interim Statement', *Proceedings of the Dorset Natural History & Archaeology Society*, 136, pp.157–61.

Ryan, M., 'The Formal Relationships of Insular Early Medieval Eucharistic Chalices', *Proceedings of the Royal Irish Academy XC(C)*, 1990, no. 10, fig. 1, p.292.

Sharp, Sheila, 'England, Europe and the Celtic World: King Athelstan's Foreign Policy', *Bulletin of the John Rylands University Library of Manchester*, 79 (3), Autumn 1997, pp.197–219.

Wood, I., 'Early Medieval Cornish pottery in Hiberno Ireland', *Cornish Archaeology*, 54, 2014, pp.223–38.

Online Resources

Nowakowski, J. and Gossip, J., 2017. Tintagel Castle, Cornwall. Archaeological Research Project TCARP16 Archive and assessment report Excavations 2016, TCARP16 (English Heritage). Available at: www.english-heritage.org.uk/siteassets/home/about-us/search-news/press-releases/press-releases-2017/tintagel-archaeology-report/3408851.pdf [Accessed 5 November 2021].

Avalon.law.yale.edu, 2008. Avalon Project: The Anglo-Saxon Chronicle. Available at: avalon.law.yale.edu/medieval/ang05.asp [Accessed 10 October 2017].

Quinnell, H., Lawson-Jones, A., Nowakowski, J., Sturge, 2007. 'Gwithian, Cornwall: Excavations 1949–1969' [data-set]. York: Archaeology Data Service [distributor]. Available at: doi.org/10.5284/1000200.

Taylor, S.R., 2017. Duckpool, Morwenstow, Cornwall. Archaeological Excavation 2017. Cornwall Council Historic Environment Service: doi.org/10.5284/1050357.

Sourcebooks.fordham.edu, 2000. Internet History Sourcebooks – Willibald's Life of St Boniface. Available at: sourcebooks.fordham.edu/basis/willibald-boniface.asp [Accessed 10 October 2017].

Exondomesday.ac.uk, 2021. Exon Domesday. Available at: www.exondomesday.ac.uk/ [Accessed 2 October 2021].

The Corpus of Anglo Saxon Stonework, 2021. The Corpus: Lanivet 3. Available at: chacklepie.com/ascorpus/catvol11.php?pageNum_urls=23&totalRows_urls=94 [Accessed 12 June 2021].

Alexander, J., 1916. The Athelstan Myth. Devon Association Transactions, pp.174–79. Available at: devonassoc.org.uk/devoninfo/the-athelstan-myth-1916/ [Accessed 5 November 2021].

Esawyer.lib.cam.ac.uk, 2022. Electronic Sawyer: The Electronic Sawyer. Available at: esawyer.lib.cam.ac.uk/

Sourcebooks.fordham.edu, 2022. The Laws of William the Conqueror. Available at: sourcebooks.fordham.edu/source/will1-lawsb.asp [Accessed 10 March 2021]

Current Archaeology, 2021. Second inscribed stone found at Tintagel – Current

Archaeology. Available at: archaeology.co.uk/articles/news/second-inscribed-stone-found-at-tintagel.htm [Accessed 15 October 2021].

Berger, D., Soles, J.S., Giumlia-Mair, A.R., Brügmann, G., Galili, E.,(2019) Isotope systematics and chemical composition of tin ingots from Mochlos (Crete) and other Late Bronze Age sites in the eastern Mediterranean Sea: An ultimate key to tin provenance?. PLOS ONE 14(6): e0218326. journals.plos.org/plosone/article?id=10.1371/journal.pone.0218326

Taylor, D., The Convert Kings: Power and Religious Affiliation in Early Anglo-Saxon England. By N. J. Higham. Book review. Journal of Church and State, 41:2, p.384. Available at: https://doi.org/10.1093/jcs/41.2.384 [Accessed 4 April 2022].

Dodd, L., 2016. 'Kinship, Conflict and Unity among Roman Elites in Post-Roman Gaul: The Contrasting Experiences of Caesarius and Avitus', in R. Varga and V. Rusu-Bolindet (eds.), Official Power and Local Elites in the Roman Provinces, pp.188–208 (Abingdon: Routledge, 2016)

Probert, Duncan. 'New Light on Aldhelm's Letter to King Gerent of Dumnonia (2010).' Aldhelm and Sherborne: Essays to Celebrate the Founding of the Bishopric (2010): n. pag. Print.

Holm, Poul. (1986). The Slave Trade of Dublin, Ninth to Twelfth Centuries. Peritia. 5. 317-345. 10.1484/J.Peri.3.139. Available at: www.researchgate.net/publication/252626663_The_Slave_Trade_of_Dublin_Ninth_to_Twelfth_Centuries

INDEX